"I've had the wonderful privilege of ministering alongside Corville Peters on AT THE CROSS Live TV, watching first-hand the richness of God's unveiled truth pouring from his heart to thousands. Now in written form, these same relevant and profound truths can be prayerfully digested. I guarantee they'll stir up your own God-given longings and deeply satisfy your soul. In this dialogue with God, you'll personally experience Christ's redemptive cross—His sacrifice, divine nature and blessings—become yours."

- Marianne Novoselac, author and recording artist,
Miracle Praise Ministries

"Reading this devotional was like taking a journey with an experienced and knowledgeable tour guide, who is more like a friend. Corville keeps both the first timer and the seasoned traveller engaged. The first timer is awestruck by his discoveries, and the seasoned traveller is amazed that he is still finding treasures in the old familiar places. To top it all off, at the end of each trip, the travellers are challenged to allow the message, work and Christ of the cross to change, strengthen, and equip them to live."

- Reverend Lennox S. John, Senior Pastor,
Faith Alive Christian Centre

CORVILLE PETERS

WHAT DOES THE CROSS MEAN TO YOU?

A Twenty-One Day Journey to Wholeness

WESTBOW
PRESS®
A DIVISION OF THOMAS NELSON
& ZONDERVAN

WestBow Press books may be ordered through booksellers or by contacting:

WestBow Press
A Division of Thomas Nelson & Zondervan
1663 Liberty Drive
Bloomington, IN 47403
www.westbowpress.com
1 (866) 928-1240

ISBN: 978-1-5127-1445-6 (sc)
ISBN: 978-1-5127-1446-3 (hc)
ISBN: 978-1-5127-1444-9 (e)

Library of Congress Control Number: 2015915976

Print information available on the last page.

WestBow Press rev. date: 11/25/2015

ACKNOWLEDGMENTS

Heavenly Father, thank you for the invaluable gift of your love demonstrated to me through the gift of your Son, Jesus Christ, His Cross and His Blood.

Lord Jesus, thank you for the gift of your Life as full payment for my sin. Thank you for dying my death and paying my sin debt.

Holy Spirit, thank you for making the power of the Cross of Jesus my daily reality through your revelation and administration.

I am ever so grateful to my wife, Martha, my daughter, Kalesha, and the AT THE CROSS Ministries family for their faithful support, as I seek to walk out the call of God on my life. I am also indebted to the many other individuals, pastors, authors, and Kingdom leaders who have in one way or another enriched my understanding and experience of the Cross of Jesus. Thank you!

CONTENTS

CONTENTS

FOREWORD

For the past twelve years, God has given me the privilege of hosting late night television call-in programs as avenues for restoring lost and broken lives through the message of the Cross of Jesus Christ. By God's grace, many have received Jesus for the first time, renewed their faith, and found strength to experience the victory that Jesus won for them at the Cross.

I have heard the desperate cries of thousands of individuals with needs running the spectrum from physical and mental health crises, emotional trauma, abuse, family disasters, broken relationships, financial ruin and legal battles, to thoughts of suicide.

Ministering to these needs, I am often reminded of the experience of Moses and the Israelites in Exodus 15:22-25. After crossing the Red Sea, they wandered about for three days without water. Finally, they found water, but it was bitter and the people named the place Marah (meaning bitter). When Moses cried out to the Lord, He showed him a tree which Moses cast into the water. The tree turned the water sweet so the people could drink it and quench their thirst.

It seems that all around, whether because of personal needs, global issues, nations at war, the fear of disease outbreaks, or natural calamities, the waters of life are becoming increasingly bitter. Desperation and hopelessness abound.

But there is good news! The tree that Moses put in the water also holds the secret for transforming the bitter waters of your circumstances and experiences, for satisfying you today, and filling you with bright hopes for tomorrow.

In the wilderness, the Lord had shown Moses a tree that was a picture of the Cross on which Jesus Christ would later bear all the sins of a fallen, helpless humanity. Hundreds of years later, on the Cross of Calvary, Jesus exchanged the bitter consequences of your and my sins for the bountiful riches God has always had in store for us.

When we were utterly helpless, Christ came at just the right time and died for us sinners. (Romans 5:6 NLT)

Whoever you are and whatever your past or present experiences, you will find true life and victory through the Cross. Understanding the truth about what the Cross of Jesus means to you will surely make all the difference in your life.

Through this book, I am delighted to journey with you to amazing discoveries, into a deeper understanding, and a richer appreciation of the person of Jesus and all He has done for you. *What Does the Cross Mean to You?* is not intended to be a comprehensive study of the Cross. Its purpose is to help you reframe the way you see the Cross, by putting the spotlight on only some of the inexhaustible blessings and benefits that God has afforded you through the finished work of the Cross of Jesus.

By the end of your Twenty-One Days Journey To Wholeness, you will come to appreciate that the Cross is not just about suffering, as is often thought. Ultimately, my goal is to encourage you to personally apply truths that will bring forth the glorious blessings of the Cross in your life.

It is my joy to welcome you to your new season of discovering, believing and receiving the gifts that Jesus purchased for you with the eternal currency of His precious Blood AT THE CROSS.

Remain in His GRIP!

Corville Peters

INTRODUCTION

The journey you are about to undertake will transform you and your future!

Amazing discoveries await you and with the Holy Spirit as your Guide, you will come away from these twenty-one days with a deeper revelation of what the Cross of Jesus means to you — personally.

Committing to this journey may very well be the most significant challenge you undertake. Why do I say this? All the good things that God has for you are yours through the Cross of Jesus. However, the truth is that you cannot possess them without a personal revelation of the meaning of the Cross and how to integrate its power in your daily life.

Through television, business, and personal relationships, I have had the privilege of meeting thousands of individuals of diverse backgrounds, religious persuasions, and social and economic status. Despite the diversity, however, there is one common denominator: everyone wants to know how to beat the odds, overcome obstacles, and live in victory.

Regardless of the circumstances you may be facing or where you are in your spiritual walk, I am fully convinced that the Cross of Jesus holds the answers you are seeking. My conviction comes out of my own personal experience and journey into the Cross. That journey began one day while driving in my car. It started with a question that broke into my consciousness: "*What does the Cross mean to you?*"

If God has ever asked you a question you know that He is about to introduce you to unknown dimensions of yourself, enlarge your understanding, and transform your perspective. God knows all things, so His questions are for our benefit not His. I have come to the conclusion that questions are God's GPS (Global Positioning System) to help us find our location in relation to Him.

We see an example of this when Adam and Eve disobeyed God and went into hiding. The first question God asked Adam, "Where are you?" (Genesis 3:9) was intended to help Adam recognize where he was spiritually. Similarly, God bombarded Job with four chapters of questions for the same purpose of bringing Job into a deeper awareness of himself in relation to God (See Job 38-41).

Unknown to me at the time, the question "*What does the Cross mean to you?*" was intended to help me track my present location in relation to the Cross of Jesus. I had already come to faith in Jesus as my Savior a few years earlier, so it seemed like a simple enough question. Without hesitation my mind formulated an answer. The Cross is the foundation of my Christian faith, because on the Cross of Calvary Jesus gave His life and shed His blood to pay for my sins.

Surprisingly, although my answer reflected Biblical truth, I was surprised to discover how limited it was.

"*That's in the past. What does the Cross mean to you today?*"

With no answer to give, in that moment I realized that I was experiencing the Cross as a historical, but not a present reality.

In the weeks and months following, I embarked on a journey to discover everything I could about the Cross. I am still on that journey of discovery; not an intellectual journey, but a journey of revelation with the Holy Spirit unveiling truth to my spirit. This journey has totally revolutionized the meaning of the Cross, from being a historical icon to becoming the divine power that shapes my life daily.

> For the message of the cross is foolishness to those
> who are perishing, but to us who are being saved
> it is the power of God. (1 Corinthians 1:18)

Today, my answer to what the Cross of Jesus means to me is very different than it was years ago. I am discovering its vast riches. I have come to realize that the Cross and its Blood are the eternal means God has provided for me to become all that He intended and for me to possess all that He has for me as His son.

First Corinthians 1:18 has opened my eyes to a new window of revelation and has ignited a passion in my heart for the message of the Cross. The message has been working deeply in my heart, to renew my mind and fill me with more of the love of Jesus. I have been consumed by an intense desire to share the "secrets" of the Cross with others, especially those who have not yet come to faith in Jesus.

God in His faithfulness soon engineered circumstances to fulfill the desire of my heart. By divine design I became a host on the CTS (Crossroads Television System) late night live call-in television program, NiteLite Live. The message of the Cross became my message and I had the joy of helping many find freedom through this unfailing source of divine power.

In 2010 the CTS NiteLite Live program ended. By then, after having hosted over two hundred programs, my passion for the message of the Cross was stronger than ever. I felt somewhat like the prophet Jeremiah. *"His word was in my heart like a burning fire shut up in my bones; I was weary of holding it back, and I could not." (Jeremiah 20:9)*

After months of prayerfully asking God for direction, I realized that the seed of the question the Lord had planted in my heart years earlier and watered through my service on NiteLite Live, was ready to be harvested. It happened a year later, in 2011, when the Lord directed me to launch AT THE CROSS Ministries and its weekly broadcast, AT THE CROSS Live TV.

I had no idea that one question could have ushered me into the depths of God's heart for lost souls and united me in such a wonderful way with His plan for my life. I believe with all my heart that this same question has the potential to birth in you a passion for the message of the Cross of Jesus and launch you into victorious living.

So, let me ask you, "What does the Cross mean to you?"

At this point in your life, The Cross of Jesus may hold little significance for you. It may just be a historical artifact, a piece of jewellery, or a religious charm to ward off evil and bring good luck. Or perhaps you are a born again believer whose experiences show little or no evidence of the Cross at work in your life.

Whatever your present view or experience of the Cross, get ready for the amazing revelation that awaits you.

PREPARING FOR THE JOURNEY

The success of any journey depends largely on preparation. The more significant the journey, the more extensive preparation becomes necessary. Certainly, one of the most important journeys you will ever take is to discover what God made possible for you at the Cross. Equally important is getting to the place where the Cross becomes your daily concentration.

This twenty-one day journey on which we are about to embark is intended to help you share the resolve of the Apostle Paul—*"For I resolved to know nothing while I was with you except Jesus Christ and him crucified."* (I Corinthians 2:2 NIV)

As you decide to concentrate on the Cross in the days ahead, you can expect to begin walking in victory, because you will be taking the truth of the Cross deep into the chamber of your heart and soul.

The main preparation for this journey is to ensure that you understand a few foundational concepts about the Cross. So, before going on to review our plan for each day, let's take a look at the concepts of divine exchange, the scope of the message of the Cross, and the Holy Spirit's witness.

DIVINE EXCHANGE

The message of the Cross is a message of divine exchange between God and humanity, with Jesus as the perfect man representing all of humanity. Because Jesus took our place, we can take His place by believing in His finished work of the Cross. These twenty-one days are opportunities to enter into the reality of what Jesus accomplished on your behalf.

Based on Derek Prince's book, *Bought With Blood: The Divine Exchange at the Cross*,[1] let me share with you a list of the nine exchanges accomplished for us by the sacrifice of Jesus on the Cross.

1. Jesus was punished that we might be FORGIVEN.
2. Jesus was wounded that we might be HEALED.
3. Jesus was made sin with our sinfulness that we might be made righteous with His RIGHTEOUSNESS.
4. Jesus died our death that we might share His LIFE.
5. Jesus was made a curse that we might share the BLESSING.
6. Jesus endured our poverty that we might share His RICHES.
7. Jesus bore our shame that we might share His GLORY.
8. Jesus endured our rejection that we might enjoy His ACCEPTANCE.
9. Our old-man died in Jesus that the NEW-MAN might live in us.

THE MESSAGE OF THE CROSS

The Cross encompasses more than the physical beams on which Jesus was crucified. The full message of the Cross includes everything that Jesus went through—the shedding of His blood, His suffering, death, burial, resurrection, and

---

[1] Derek Prince, Bought With Blood: The Divine Exchange at the Cross, (Grand Rapids, MI: Chosen Books, 2007)

ascension. Everything that Jesus experienced at each stage is wrapped up in the finished work of the Cross. So bear in mind that expressions such as *At the Cross* and *The Cross of Jesus* are not limited to the place of Jesus' crucifixion. They are meant to capture the totality of all that Jesus accomplished and endured to fulfill God's redemptive plan for humanity.

As believers in Christ, we are meant to experience the resurrection power of Jesus in our lives. However, many would prefer to bypass the Cross, which is God's altar for the death of a self-centered life in exchange for the resurrected spirit life. The Apostle Paul's desire ought to be ours as well.

> *"I want to know Christ and experience the mighty power that raised him from the dead. I want to suffer with him, sharing in his death." (Philippians 3:10 NLT)*

HOLY SPIRIT'S WITNESS

We don't usually hear much about the Holy Spirit's involvement in the finished work of the Cross. However, both the sacrificial offering of Jesus' life and the application of His accomplishments to our lives are by the power of the Holy Spirit.

> *"For by the power of the eternal Spirit, Christ offered himself to God as a perfect sacrifice for our sins." (Hebrews 9:14 NLT)*

> *"This is He who came by water and blood—Jesus Christ; not only by water, but by water and blood. And it is the Spirit who bears witness, because the Spirit is truth. For there are three that bear witness in heaven: the Father, the Word, and the Holy*

> *Spirit; and these three are one. And there are three*
> *that bear witness on earth: the Spirit, the water,*
> *and the blood; and these three agree as one." (I*
> *John 5:6-8)*

According to Andrew Murray, through this unity between the Holy Spirit and the blood of the Cross, "God has provided that the blood, as a vital power, automatically and ceaselessly carries on its work within us."[1] Hallelujah!

So, throughout the journey, you will want to remain conscious of the Holy Spirit, not only as Guide, but as the One who reveals truth and applies it to your life

THE DAILY PLAN

The daily plan for our Twenty One Day journey includes the following:

1. *Key Word and Scripture*: The key word and Scripture describe a benefit or blessing you receive AT THE CROSS. The effect of the benefit or blessing is reinforced by a personalized phrase. For example, AT THE CROSS *I am Loved.* AT THE CROSS *I receive Grace.* AT THE CROSS *I find Peace.*

2. *Insights and Thoughts*: In this segment, insights and thoughts elaborate on the day's benefit or blessing. The goal of this segment is to heighten your awareness of what the Cross means to you. To the extent there is duplication, it is good to reinforce these fundamental concepts.

---

[1] Andrew Murray, The Blood of the Cross, (New Kensington, PA: Whitaker House, 1981), p.9.

3. *Personal Application*: This practical part of each day's journey gives you the opportunity to concentrate on the divine exchange of the Cross in a personal way. In Luke 9:23, Jesus invites a *daily* taking up of our cross, which essentially involves exchanging our natural self-orientation and expressions for His Spirit-centered life. Surrender is not a pleasant word for most of us. However, unless we are willing to enter into this exchange, the power of the Cross will have little effect upon our lives. The personal application exercise helps you to be a doer of the Word and not only a hearer. (James 1: 22-24) Take a few minutes and journal whatever the Holy Spirit brings to your attention.

4. *Faith Confession*: A simple verbal declaration that releases supernatural faith to align your thoughts with the revealed truths.

5. *Prayer*: Each day's encounter includes a short prayer, which can be expanded or modified as you see fit. Also, pray the words, don't just read them. Because of what the Cross and blood of Jesus have accomplished on your behalf, you can confidently approach God as your Heavenly Father. Go boldly with thanksgiving and receive what He has for you.

6. *A Deeper Look Through the Window of Truth*: Finally, you'll find a collection of Scripture verses related to the subject of the day. Meditating on these verses through the day will certainly give you a richer appreciation of the person of Jesus and His finished work.

May God bless you with amazing discoveries and revelation. May He also establish you in the truths you discover on this journey.

Day 1

I am

Loved

For God so loved the world that He gave His only begotten Son,
that whoever believes in Him should not perish
but have everlasting life.
John 3:16

Did you know that you were created for love and you exist because of love? I mean Divine Love. It's a category of love all by itself, distinct from every form of human love.

Creator God is Love, and His Divine Love in action brought forth human beings out of Himself (1 John 4:8; Genesis 1:26-27). God created all of humanity in Adam, and when Adam sinned all humanity experienced spiritual death or separation from God (Genesis 2-3).

Having succeeded in getting Adam and Eve to disobey God's command, Satan thought this was the end. He was wrong! He thought that the relationship between God and His family of human offspring was over. He expected God to give up on humanity and turn His back on us the way we had turned our backs on Him. Truth be told, satan really had no idea of God's boundless, unchanging, unconditional love, which never gives up and never runs out. This is Divine Love which gives and keeps on giving.

Satan did not realize that Divine Love had already anticipated and met the need of fallen humanity. He did not know that through the blood sacrifice of Jesus, the innocent Lamb of God slain from the foundation of the world, Divine Love had already made provision to once for all pay for our sin and bring us back from death to life.

My friend, God has always loved you and will always love you! If you are having trouble believing and receiving God's love for you, or if you desire to grow deeper in God's love, take a close look at how God showed His love for you at the Cross.

> *"For when we were still without strength, in due time Christ died for the ungodly. For scarcely for a righteous man will one die; yet perhaps for a good man someone would even dare to die. But God demonstrates His own love toward us, in that while we were still sinners, Christ died for us."* (Romans 5:6-8)

There you have it! Proof of the ultimate demonstration of God's love for you!

The movie, *Passion of the Christ*, portrayed the brutal scourging and whipping that Jesus endured. Although some have said the scenes were too graphic, I want you to know that what the movie depicted is only a fraction of what Divine Love chose to endure to win you back. This is how the prophet Isaiah described what he saw through the Spirit years before Jesus was born: *"But many were amazed when they saw him. His face was so disfigured he seemed hardly human, and from his appearance, one would scarcely know he was a man." (Isaiah 52:14 NLT)*

Don't make the mistake others have made by thinking that your bad experiences and lingering problems are proof that God does not love you. That is one of the biggest lies Satan will use to drive a wedge in your relationship with God.

Here's a question from God's Word that will set your perspective straight. *"Since he did not spare even his own Son but gave him up for us all, won't he also give us everything else?" (Romans 8:32 NLT)*

I pray that you will believe the truth of God's Word, rather than the lies of satan, that you will trust God's goodness and confidently wait on His perfect timing to answer your prayers.

For the rest of your days may you remember that first and foremost the Cross means you are unconditionally loved by God, your Creator and Heavenly Father.

PERSONAL APPLICATION

What misconceptions about God's love for you do you need to exchange at the Cross?

_____

_____

_____

_____

_____

_____

_____

FAITH CONFESSION

God loves me personally not because of what I do, but because of what Jesus has accomplished for me. God's love for me is pure, rich, vast, unconditional and everlasting. Nothing will ever separate me from the love God has demonstrated for me at the Cross.

PRAYER

Heavenly Father, thank you for your great love that will never give up or run out on me. I open my heart to receive a greater revelation of the love you have for me personally. In spite of my circumstances, I choose to believe that your perfect love will ultimately work all things in my life for my good. Let my heart be established today in your perfect love, so that every kind of fear is cast out of my life. Amen.

A DEEPER LOOK THROUGH THE WINDOW OF TRUTH

- *But God is so rich in mercy, and he loved us so much, that even though we were dead because of our sins, he gave us life when he raised Christ from the dead. (Ephesians 2: 4-5 NLT)*
- *See what great love the Father has lavished on us, that we should be called children of God! And that is what we are! (1 John 3:1 NIV)*
- *For we know how dearly God loves us, because he has given us the Holy Spirit to fill our hearts with his love. (Romans 5:5 NLT)*
- *Such love has no fear, because perfect love expels all fear. If we are afraid, it is for fear of punishment, and this shows that we have not fully experienced his perfect love. (1 John 4:18 NLT)*

- *Can anything ever separate us from Christ's love? Does it mean he no longer loves us if we have trouble or calamity, or are persecuted, or hungry, or destitute, or in danger, or threatened with death? (As the Scriptures say, "For your sake we are killed every day; we are being slaughtered like sheep.") No, despite all these things, overwhelming victory is ours through Christ, who loved us. And I am convinced that nothing can ever separate us from God's love. Neither death nor life, neither angels nor demons, neither our fears for today nor our worries about tomorrow—not even the powers of hell can separate us from God's love. No power in the sky above or in the earth below—indeed, nothing in all creation will ever be able to separate us from the love of God that is revealed in Christ Jesus our Lord. (Romans 8:35-39)*

Day 2

AT THE CROSS

I am

Accepted

*To the praise of the glory of His grace,
by which He made us accepted in the Beloved.*
Ephesians 1:6 KJV

To the extent you are assured of God's perfect love for you, you will be assured of His acceptance.

Some of the most heart-wrenching calls I have received on our call-in television program are directly or indirectly related to rejection in childhood or later years. Many of the issues have been further complicated by addictions to substances and unhealthy lifestyles used as remedies for the pain of addiction. My prayer for each one is that they would recognize that the only remedy for rejection is found in the Cross of Jesus.

The Cross means acceptance because Jesus experienced rejection and abandonment in our place that we might enjoy His acceptance. In His piercing cry from the Cross, *"My God, my God, why have you forsaken me?"* (Matthew 27:46) We hear the anguish Jesus felt in being deserted by His Father for the first time, as He took the sins of all humanity upon Himself.

Because Jesus was forsaken, God will never forsake you (Hebrews 13:5). In the Old Testament sacrifice of the burnt offering, you will see a picture of your acceptance in Christ.

> *"Then he shall put his hand on the head of the burnt offering, and it will be accepted on his behalf to make atonement for him." (Leviticus 1:4)*

Jesus' perfect sacrifice has been accepted on your behalf and, in exchange, His acceptance has been transferred to you. Your Heavenly Father's unshakeable acceptance is yours to enjoy by putting your faith in the finished work of the Cross.

Let's now take another look at today's key verse: *"To the praise of the glory of His grace, by which He made us accepted in the Beloved."* Your acceptance in Jesus Christ, the Beloved, is praiseworthy as the pinnacle accomplishment of God's great (weighty) grace. By what process did grace make you accepted? The passage from which our key verse is taken (Ephesians 1:3-7) and other verses in the New Testament give us some insights.

Chosen: First God chose us in Christ before time began. He knew we would sin, yet He looked out in time beyond the Cross and saw us holy and blameless because of Jesus' sacrifice on our behalf. (Ephesians 1:4)

Adopted: God decided in advance to adopt us into His own family through Jesus Christ. (Ephesians 1:5; Galatians 4:4-5)

Forgiven: With the currency of His rich grace, and the precious blood of His Son, God purchased our freedom (redeemed us) and forgave our sins. (Ephesians 1:7)

Access & Belonging: The Blood of the Cross of Jesus opened the way for us to draw near to God, enter the holiest place, freely access the throne of grace, and find the place we belong in the household of God. (Hebrews 10:19-20; Ephesians 2:13,19)

Raised Up: Because of His great love and rich mercy, God made us alive with Christ, raised us up with Him and made us sit together in the heavenly realms in Christ. That's sharing in Jesus' resurrection and ascension; a blessing and privilege that surely demonstrates God's acceptance! (Ephesians 2:5-6)

Indwelling Presence: By the power of the Blood of the Cross that cleanses and purified us, we become a suitable temple for the Holy God. The ultimate mark of our acceptance to God is having the indwelling presence of the Father and the Son through the Holy Spirit. (John 14: 17, 23)

Blessed: God the Father blessed us in the heavenly realms with every spiritual blessing in Christ. (Ephesians 1:3) As Christ is blessed so are we, because His acceptance is transferred to us.

You will agree that these seven actions of God are undeniable evidence of your acceptance.

PERSONAL APPLICATION

What do you need to exchange at the Cross today to rest in the assurance that you are accepted in Christ?

_____

_____

_____

_____

_____

_____

FAITH CONFESSION

When the Father sees me in Christ, He accepts me the same way He accepts Christ.

PRAYER

Heavenly Father, thank you for judging my sins in the body of Jesus, so that today your anger and wrath are turned away from me. Thank you for showing me the plan you had for my life even before time began. It is wonderful to know that I am accepted in Christ and you see me clothed in His righteousness and perfection. Help me to believe with all my heart that because of what Jesus did for me at the Cross you will never turn your back on me.

A DEEPER LOOK THROUGH THE WINDOW OF TRUTH

- *For He [God] Himself has said, I will not in any way fail you nor give you up nor leave you without support. [I will] not, [I will] not, [I will] not in any degree leave you helpless nor forsake nor let [you] down (relax My hold on you)! [Assuredly not!]. (Hebrews 13:5b AMP)*
- *But now in Christ Jesus you who once were far off have been brought near by the blood of Christ... Now, therefore, you are no longer strangers and foreigners, but fellow citizens with the saints and members of the household of God. (Ephesians 2:13, 19)*
- *For by one offering He has perfected forever those who are being sanctified... Therefore, brethren, having boldness to enter the Holiest by the blood of Jesus. (Hebrews 10:14, 19)*
- *Therefore, accept each other just as Christ has accepted you so that God will be given glory. (Romans 15:7 NLT)*

Day 3

AT THE CROSS

I receive

Grace

For by grace you have been saved through faith, and that
not of yourselves; it is the gift of God.
Ephesians 2:8

Like the Cross, Grace is one of those words that means different things to different individuals. For some it is a prayer said before eating a meal, for others it is a licence to sin or a doctrine that divides the church.

So let's clarify what we mean by grace. Grace is God's unmerited favor which we cannot earn and which we do not deserve. Unmerited favor is not just for acquiring material possessions or for receiving preferential treatment from others. The unmerited favor of God describes how God relates to us based on what Jesus did for us at the Cross.

On the basis of Ephesians 2:8, most believers would agree that salvation is a work of grace. Titus 2:11 also makes it very clear: *"The grace of God that brings salvation has appeared to all men."*

This saving grace appeared in a man, Jesus, and was made available to us through His finished work at the Cross. Grace accomplished what the law could not do.

> "And of His fullness we have all received, and grace for grace For the law was given through Moses, but grace and truth came through Jesus Christ." (John 1:16-17)

> "For what the law was powerless to do because it was weakened by the flesh, God did by sending his own Son in the likeness of sinful flesh to be a sin offering. And so he condemned sin in the flesh." (Romans 8:3 NIV)

The good news message of the Cross is that with His blood Jesus mediated a new covenant of grace on behalf of all humanity. This new covenant of grace is not licence to sin, as some may believe. Rather, it gives us the assurance that God's grace is always greater than every sin and is always available to give us victory over sin.

To better appreciate the full effect of the grace received at the Cross, it is important to understand that being saved by grace is not limited to your initial salvation experience. The Greek word for saved, "sozo" also includes healing, deliverance, prosperity and everything else that encompasses your total wellbeing as intended by God.

The same grace by which you receive your initial salvation experience is the same grace by which you continue to live out your Christian experience. It is a mistake to think that grace worked only up to the point of your initial salvation, but left you on your own to figure out how to keep sin out of your life afterwards. It doesn't work that way. You started out by grace and you continue by grace.

I minister to countless individuals, helping them to see that their victory lies in receiving the kindness God has shown them through the Cross. For believers in Christ, I also help them to see that the secret to victorious Christian living is the daily surrender of their self-effort at the altar of the Cross in exchange for God's grace.

Today, God wants to point to you and me as *"Examples of the incredible wealth of his grace and kindness shown toward us."* (Ephesians 2:7 NLT)

I want God to look at my life and see me living by grace, rather than relying on my own efforts to be accepted by Him.

Getting to the place of having the grace of God overflow in our lives requires that we know how to access grace. Romans 5:2 tells us we gain access to grace by faith and according to Romans 12:3, God has given us the measure of faith necessary to access His grace. Let us release the faith God gives us and see His multi-faceted grace work in every area of our lives for His glory. (1 Peter 4:10)

PERSONAL APPLICATION

What do you need to exchange at the Cross today for God's grace to do its work in your life?

_____

_____

_____

_____

_____

_____

FAITH CONFESSION

At the Cross I receive the incredible wealth of God's grace and kindness, which is at work in every area of my life. I live by faith in God's grace.

PRAYER

Heavenly Father, thank you for your new covenant of grace that has freed me from self-effort. Help me by your Holy Spirit to continue believing and living by your grace. I am full of joy knowing that because of the precious blood of Jesus offered on my behalf, I can come boldly to your throne of grace to present my needs and the needs of others. Above all, I can come boldly to your throne with my praise and adoration for all you have already done for me.

A DEEPER LOOK THROUGH THE WINDOW OF TRUTH

- *For all have sinned and fall short of the glory of God, being justified freely by His grace through the redemption that is in Christ Jesus. (Romans 3:23-24)*
- *For sin shall not have dominion over you, for you are not under law but under grace. (Romans 6:14)*
- *Moreover the law entered that the offense might abound. But where sin abounded, grace abounded much more. (Romans 5:20)*
- *For you know the grace of our Lord Jesus Christ, that though He was rich, yet for your sakes He became poor, that you through His poverty might become rich. (2 Corinthians 8:9)*
- *And He said to me, "My grace is sufficient for you, for My strength is made perfect in weakness." Therefore most gladly I will rather boast in my infirmities, that the power of Christ may rest upon me. (2 Corinthians 12:9)*

- *For we do not have a High Priest who cannot sympathize with our weaknesses, but was in all points tempted as we are, yet without sin. Let us therefore come boldly to the throne of grace, that we may obtain mercy and find grace to help in time of need. (Hebrews 4:15-16)*

Day 4

AT THE CROSS

I receive

Mercy

But God, who is rich in mercy,
because of His great love with which He loved us.
Ephesians 2:4

You and I have no way of fully grasping the richness of God's mercy, but our appreciation will certainly deepen as we discover more of what happened at the Cross. As our key verse tells us, God's mercy flows out of His great love for us. Mercy is the fruit of Divine Love expressed at the Cross. Mercy is God's lovingkindness.

Mercy and grace go hand in hand like two sides of the same coin. Mercy does not give us what we deserve, while grace gives us what we do not deserve. We cannot get away from appreciating God's great love for us because it is indeed the fountain head of His mercy, grace and everything else that we receive through the Cross of Jesus.

God in His holiness must judge and punish sin, so it is only because of the Cross that we can receive grace and mercy. At the Cross Jesus paid for our sins with His blood and took the punishment we deserved.

So what does the Cross mean to you? It means that mercy triumphed over judgment. (James 2:13 NIV) It means that Jesus took the judgment due you, that you may receive God's rich mercy in exchange.

On God's part, He relates to you through Jesus' perfect sacrifice. On your part, the way you relate to God will depend largely on whether or not you believe that God loves you enough to show you His mercy.

God's mercy is indeed available to you and extended to you! All you have to do is believe that Jesus became sin for you and that with His blood He paid for every sin you will ever commit in your lifetime. In fact, as it was in Old Testament times when the priests sprinkled the mercy seat with the sacrificial blood of animals (Leviticus 16:15-17), Jesus, the Great High Priest, has sprinkled the heavenly mercy seat with His own Blood.

The sprinkled blood of Jesus has accomplished an eternal covering and redemption for you, and forever speaks good things on your behalf. Abel's blood that was spilled by His brother, Cain, cried out for vengeance. Jesus' blood that was poured out for you cries mercy and intercedes on your behalf.

> *"But you have come... to Jesus the mediator of*
> *a new covenant, and to the sprinkled blood that*
> *speaks a better word than the blood of Abel."*
> *(Hebrews 12:22a, 24)*

There is no need to struggle anymore. Approach God today in confidence and with full assurance that the blood of Jesus qualifies you to receive His mercy. You can believe that in God's love, mercy and grace, His goodness is poured out to meet your every need.

Hebrews 8:12 is a verse that could be considered God's antidote for condemnation, unworthiness and every other feeling that would keep you from God.

> *"For I will be merciful to their unrighteousness, and their sins and their lawless deeds I will remember no more."*

God is not like man. God says, *"I will be merciful"* and you can count on Him keeping His Word! Faith in the Blood of the Cross releases God's mercy to permanently override all unrighteousness—all our sins and lawless deeds. This act of mercy also applies to whatever unrighteousness may be at work in our lives from inherited generational legacies. Because of the blood, God says He will remember them no more.

This is what it means in practical terms to be justified—having a clean slate with God, just as if you had never sinned.

> *"Much more then, having now been justified by His blood, we shall be saved from wrath through Him."*
> *(Romans 5:9)*

> *"So now, since we have been made right in God's sight by faith in his promises, we can have real peace with him because of what Jesus Christ our Lord has done for us." (Romans 5:1 TLB)*

Do you see what mercy did for you through faith in the finished work and blood of the Cross? It rescued you from God's wrath, anger and condemnation, and it gave you real peace with God instead. How amazing is God's mercy!

My friend, God's mercy means total forgiveness without recall. Why don't you embrace this rich blessing today by forgetting what mercy has forgotten and remember, what God's grace (unmerited favor) has given you.

PERSONAL APPLICATION

What do you need to exchange at the Cross today to embrace God's rich mercy?

_____

_____

_____

_____

_____

_____

_____

FAITH CONFESSION

I am confident that because of Jesus' sacrifice for me on the Cross, the full benefit of God's mercy is extended to me.

PRAYER

Heavenly Father, thank you for showing me such rich mercy that through the blood of the Cross you have not only forgiven, but forgotten everything that would prevent me from freely coming into your presence. Help me to develop a new consciousness of this mercy that is always at work in my life, freeing me to enjoy the blessings of your grace. Thank you for the blood of Jesus that speaks good things about me in your presence day and night. Amen.

A DEEPER LOOK THROUGH THE WINDOW OF TRUTH

- *The LORD is merciful and gracious, slow to anger, and abounding in mercy. (Psalm 103:8)*
- *But when God our Savior revealed his kindness and love, he saved us, not because of the righteous things we had done, but because of his mercy. He washed away our sins, giving us a new birth and new life through the Holy Spirit. He generously poured out the Spirit upon us through Jesus Christ our Savior. (Titus 3:4-6 NLT)*
- *Let us therefore come boldly to the throne of grace that we may obtain mercy and find grace to help in time of need. (Hebrews 4:16)*
- *Once you had no identity as a people; now you are God's people. Once you received no mercy; now you have received God's mercy. (1 Peter 2:10 NLT)*
- *Therefore be merciful, just as your Father also is merciful. (Luke 6:36)*

Day 5

AT THE CROSS

I am

Forgiven

When you were dead in your sins and in the uncircumcision
of your flesh, God made you alive with Christ.
He forgave us all our sins.
Colossians 2:13 NIV

We began our journey with the benefit of being loved unconditionally by God, because love is the ultimate message of the Cross. Today we focus on the benefit of being forgiven. Next to embracing God's unconditional love, your acceptance of the complete forgiveness that Jesus paid for you at the Cross with His shed Blood, is the key to enjoying the other benefits of the Cross.

The little word "**all**" in Colossians 2:13 have profound importance. It covers every sin you have committed or will ever commit: past, present and future. If you can think for a moment of someone fully paying a debt on your behalf that you could never possibly pay, then you will begin to grasp the magnitude of what the forgiveness of the Cross means to you.

Jesus' payment of your and my sin debt was so complete it even included advance payment for every sin not yet committed. That is quite amazing!

> *"Behold! The Lamb of God who takes away the sin of the world!" (John 1:29)*

The Bible tells us that there is no forgiveness without the shedding of blood. (Hebrews 9:22; Leviticus 17:11). In Old Testament times, the high priest continually offered the sacrifice of the blood of innocent animals for his own sins and the sins of the people. But these sacrifices had limited application, for they had to be offered again and again. However, when Jesus as the High Priest of our salvation sacrificed His life and His blood at the Cross, it was "once for all." (Hebrews 7:27)

Jesus' perfect sacrifice paid for our complete forgiveness, but it does not give us the licence to sin or ignore the need for the cleansing blood of Jesus to be applied to our lives when we sin.

> *"If we confess our sins, he is faithful and just to forgive our sins, and to cleanse us from all unrighteousness." (1 John 1:9)*

To be forgiven, you believe in Jesus' perfect sacrifice for your sins and the divine exchange of Him taking your punishment. This is the door to your initial salvation experience. But it does not end there. Believing that you are completely forgiven is also the secret to living your Christian life with confidence and growing into spiritual maturity. Here is why: being certain of your forgiveness through the divine exchange of the Cross empowers and enables you, to live free from guilt, condemnation, shame and fear of judgment; to approach God as your Father with confidence; to believe for God's goodness to be released into your life; and to love much.

Did you know that your love for Jesus is directly linked to what you believe about your forgiveness? Look at Luke 7:47. *"He who has been forgiven little loves little."* What was Jesus saying? Not that God ever forgives little, but how much we believe we need to be forgiven, or have been forgiven by God, is the measure to which we will love God.

My friend, let's not fool ourselves. We have been forgiven much because of the blood and divine exchange of the Cross!

PERSONAL APPLICATION

What do you need to exchange at the Cross today to enjoy the fruit of God's complete forgiveness?

_____

_____

_____

_____

_____

_____

FAITH CONFESSION

AT THE CROSS I am totally forgiven by the Blood of Jesus, which was offered once for all my sins. I forgive others as God has forgiven me.

PRAYER

Heavenly Father, I am grateful for the gift of your Son, Jesus, and His payment in full for all my sins. Thank you for accepting Jesus' perfect sacrifice on my behalf. I ask you to give me a deeper revelation and appreciation of your total forgiveness. I want to know in my heart how much I have been forgiven, so I can love much and be free from guilt, condemnation, shame and fear. Help me each day to fix my gaze upon Jesus, the Lamb of God, who takes away the sins of the world, instead of focusing on the weaknesses and shortcomings I see in myself. Amen.

A DEEPER LOOK THROUGH THE WINDOW OF TRUTH

- *In Him we have redemption through His blood, the forgiveness of sins, according to the riches of His grace. (Ephesians 1:7)*
- *And since we have been made right in God's sight by the blood of Christ, he will certainly save us from God's condemnation. (Romans 5:9 NLT)*
- *This is my blood of the covenant, which is poured out for many for the forgiveness of sins. (Matthew 26:28)*
- *You were dead because of your sins and because your sinful nature was not yet cut away. Then God made you alive with Christ, for he forgave all our sins. He cancelled the record of the charges against us and took it away by nailing it to the cross. (Colossians 2:13-14 NLT)*
- *Bear with each other and forgive one another if any of you has a grievance against someone. Forgive as the Lord forgave you. And over all these virtues put on love, which binds them all together in perfect unity. (Colossians 3:13-14 NIV)*

Day 6

AT THE CROSS

I am

Cleansed

But if we walk in the light as He is in the light,
we have fellowship with one another, and
the blood of Jesus Christ His Son cleanses us from all sin.
I John 1:7

Today's good news is that through the Blood of the Cross of Jesus you are not only forgiven, you are cleansed!

I have heard individuals say that they know God has forgiven their sins, yet they lack the confidence to approach God. How can that be? Part of the problem stems from not realizing that the blood of Jesus has also cleansed them.

In addition to separating us from God, sin contaminates our whole being, including our thought life. By His grace, God has provided for both the blotting out of our sin and removal of the effects sin has on us. Forgiveness blots out the actual sin before God, while cleansing frees us from the condemnation, guilt, and all the unrighteousness that sin produces. Forgiveness opens the way for right relationship with a holy God, while cleansing gives us the confidence to approach God without fear, to serve and worship Him.

> *"Just think how much more the blood of Christ will purify our consciences from sinful deeds so that we can worship the living God. For by the power of the eternal Spirit, Christ offered himself to God as a perfect sacrifice for our sins." (Hebrews 9:14 NLT)*

To cleanse means to purge and to remove impurities, including stains and dirt. By the purging and purifying of your conscience, the cleansing blood of Jesus removes the aroma, trace, memory, and impression of sin. As you experience this perfect work of the Cross, your consciousness of what Jesus has done for you will be greater than your consciousness of the sins you have or could commit. This does not mean you ignore sin in your life. By no means. However, by concentrating on what the Cross has done in you and for you, the tendency to sin will grow weaker and weaker.

Well, what happens when we sin? We humbly acknowledge the sin before God and sincerely repent knowing, that Jesus has already offered His blood as the perfect payment for our forgiveness and cleansing.

> *"If we confess our sins, he is faithful and just to forgive our sins, and to cleanse us from all unrighteousness." (1 John 1:9)*

Confessing or telling God about our sins is important, but that is not what frees us from guilt. Only the blood of the Cross does that. So when we confess our sins, we put our faith in the finished work of Jesus to activate the forgiveness and cleansing that we have already received at the Cross.

31

Jesus actually offered up Himself as a sacrifice to accomplish your cleansing, and when you put your faith in Him, you actually share His place in God's presence.

> *"When He had by offering Himself accomplished our cleansing of sins and riddance of guilt, He sat down at the right hand of the divine Majesty on high." (Hebrews 1:3b AMP)*

> *"And God raised us up with Christ and seated us with him in the heavenly realms in Christ Jesus." (Ephesians 2:6 NIV)*

The cleansing blood of Jesus also strengthens you against Satan's accusations. My friend, when you live with the consciousness that you are cleansed by the Blood of the Cross, nothing will make you feel that you are not worthy of being in God's presence.

Did you notice that the key verse for today, 1 John 1:7, links "fellowship with one another" to cleansing? Could this verse hold the answer for individuals who may have, for one reason or another, given up on meeting with fellow believers in the church? (Hebrews 10:25) When we experience the purifying power of the cleansing Blood of the Cross, it removes the contamination from every source that could separate us from fellowship with God and each other.

Leprosy in the Bible is a picture of the contamination of sin. In Leviticus 14, under the Old Covenant, God provided a purification process for lepers to be cleansed and restored to communal fellowship. How much more then shall the New Covenant blood of Jesus purify and restore us to full fellowship with God and others. What Jesus did for the leper in the gospels, He did for you at the Cross. His outstretched hands touched you, and He pronounced over you, "*I am willing; be cleansed.*" (Mark 1:41)

There are three that agree and bear witness to your cleansing: the water (of the Word), the Spirit, and the Blood. (1 John 5:8) When you come to faith in Jesus, the eternal Spirit lives in you to accomplish your continual cleansing by the Blood and the Word.

"*You are already **clean** because of the word which I have spoken to you.*" (John 15:3) These are the very words of Jesus. You'll find them in red in most Bibles. All you have to do is believe and receive!

PERSONAL APPLICATION

What do you need to exchange at the Cross today to experience the cleansing power of the Blood of the Cross?

_____

_____

_____

_____

_____

_____

_____

_____

FAITH CONFESSION

I am cleansed by the purifying blood of Jesus and the water of the Word of God. My conscience is purged and I am free to experience the nearness of God.

PRAYER

Heavenly Father, thank you for cleansing me from the impurities of sin through the Blood of Jesus and your Word. I believe your Word that because of Jesus' finished work you have lifted me up into your presence with Jesus Christ. Thank you for your Holy Spirit who is always at work making the blood of the Cross and your Word effective in my life. I rejoice today that because my conscience is purged from evil nothing separates me from fellowship with you and other believers in Christ. Amen.

A DEEPER LOOK THROUGH THE WINDOW OF TRUTH

- *Purge me with hyssop, and I shall be clean; Wash me, and I shall be whiter than snow. Do not cast me away from Your presence, And do not take Your Holy Spirit from me. (Psalm 51:7,11)*
- *For if the blood of bulls and goats and the ashes of a heifer, sprinkling the unclean, sanctifies for the purifying of the flesh, [14] how much more shall the blood of Christ, who through the eternal Spirit offered Himself without spot to God, cleanse your conscience from dead works to serve the living God? (Hebrews 9:13-14)*
- *And so, dear brothers and sisters, we can boldly enter heaven's Most Holy Place because of the Blood of Jesus. By his death, Jesus opened a new and life-giving way through the curtain into the Most Holy Place. And since we have a*

great High Priest who rules over God's house, let us go right into the presence of God with sincere hearts fully trusting him. For our guilty consciences have been sprinkled with Christ's Blood to make us clean, and our bodies have been washed with pure water. (Hebrews 10:19-22 NLT)

- *Christ loved the church and gave himself up for her to make her holy, cleansing her by the washing with water through the word, and to present her to himself as a radiant church, without stain or wrinkle or any other blemish, but holy and blameless. (Ephesians 5:25-27 NIV)*

Day 7

I am

Redeemed

*Christ has redeemed us from the curse of the law,
having become a curse for us (for it is written,
"Cursed is everyone who hangs on a tree").*
Galatians 3:13

Over the past two days, we explored the benefits of forgiveness
and cleansing from sin that Jesus paid for us through HIs Blood.
Today, we look at the benefit of being redeemed from the
curse. To experience life as one who has been redeemed at
the Cross, it is important that you understand what it means
to be redeemed, and how Jesus accomplished this work on
your behalf.

The words redeemed and redemption, convey the
concept of payment, exchange and repossession. It is regaining
possession of something valuable in exchange for a payment.
To see more clearly how this applies to you, may I invite you
to imagine this scene with me for a moment.

Picture human beings on a trading block, paraded before

potential buyers and auctioned like animals or merchandise. The conditions are deplorable. Extreme terror and pandemonium fill the atmosphere. The treatment is sub-human; individuals chained, beaten and shoved around. Humans created by God in His glorious image now totally helpless; stripped of all dignity, honor and freedom.

That is the scene of a slave market and our former spiritual condition because of sin. According to Romans 7:14, we were "sold under sin"—doomed in Satan's captivity, shoved from one form of bondage to another, separated from God, and bearing the curse of sin upon our heads.

Now think of Jesus going to the Cross, the agonizing suffering, His Blood being poured out and his broken body hanging on the Cross like a wretched criminal. All the time He was carrying out the legal transaction necessary to purchase you and me out of the slavery of sin, paying the price with the currency of His precious Blood. Have you ever wondered how they could have inflicted such brutality upon Jesus. No need to wonder anymore. No one did it to Him. He deliberately endured it all, to redeem your life and mine.

Today's key verse tells us that Jesus redeemed us from the curse of the law. How did He do that? He became a curse for us when He hung on the Cross. Death by any other means would not have destroyed the curse that was upon you and me as a result of having broken God's law. But Jesus endured the Cross because He knew the word of Deuteronomy 21:23: "...*he who is hanged is accursed of God.*" He actually took our place and was cursed for us.

Before Jesus hung on the Cross, it was no more than an instrument of torturous and shameful death for criminals. But the Cross of Jesus was not a mere instrument of torture and death. It was God's pre-ordained instrument of redemption.

One of the two thieves hanging on either side of Jesus was the first to receive that revelation. Remember what Jesus pledged to him in response to his request for Jesus to remember him: *"Today you will be with me in paradise."* (Luke 23:43) You and I can also experience the redemptive power that God invested in the Cross when we believe in its finished work.

When you put your faith in the finished work of the Cross, you experience the divine exchange that Jesus accomplished on your behalf: the blessing instead of the curse.

- For sickness He has given you health.
- For poverty He has given you prosperity.
- For death He has given you spiritual life.

Deuteronomy 28 describes what it means to be redeemed from the curse of the law. Fourteen verses of that Chapter contain blessing, while fifty-four contain curses as devastating consequences of disobedience. At the Cross Jesus took every single curse upon Himself (including ones not listed), became a curse for us, and engineered a priceless divine exchange. Through this exchange, Jesus' perfect obedience was imputed to us. We were transferred out of the curse that we might share in the blessing.

I'd say this is a good place to shout, "Hallelujah!"

Regardless of what condition of the curse may still be at work in your life, I encourage you to anchor your faith in Jesus' perfect redemptive work and continually pronounce over yourself that you are the redeemed of the Lord. In time, your faith will break through and you can expect to see the blessings of the Cross manifested in your life and circumstances.

PERSONAL APPLICATION

What kind of curse do you need to exchange at the Cross today to enter into the experience of being redeemed by the blood and Cross of Jesus?

_____

_____

_____

_____

_____

_____

_____

FAITH CONFESSION

Every curse in my life is destroyed because Jesus became a curse for me on the Cross. I am redeemed from all curses.

PRAYER

Heavenly Father, I thank you for sending Jesus to redeem me with His blood and by hanging on a Cross. I thank you that Jesus accomplished all that was necessary to rescue me out of satan's slave market and break every curse that was operating in my life. I receive my full and complete freedom from every kind of curse and I ask that the redeeming Blood of Jesus be applied to my family, to destroy every family-related or generational curse. Amen.

A DEEPER LOOK THROUGH THE WINDOW OF TRUTH

- *Has the LORD redeemed you? Then speak out! Tell others he has redeemed you from your enemies. (Psalm 107:2 NLT)*

- *You are worthy to take the scroll, And to open its seals; for You were slain, And have redeemed us to God by Your blood out of every tribe and tongue and people and nation. (Revelation 5:9)*

- *Giving thanks to the Father who has qualified us to be partakers of the inheritance of the saints in the light. He has delivered us from the power of darkness and conveyed us into the kingdom of the Son of His love, in whom we have redemption through His blood, the forgiveness of sins. (Colossians 1:12-14)*

- *Bless the Lord, O my soul; And all that is within me, bless His holy name! Who redeems your life from destruction, who crowns you with lovingkindness and tender mercies. (Psalm 103: 1,4)*

- *Don't you realize that you become the slave of whatever you choose to obey? You can be a slave to sin, which leads to death, or you can choose to obey God, which leads to righteous living. Thank God! Once you were slaves of sin, but now you wholeheartedly obey this teaching we have given you. Now you are free from your slavery to sin, and you have become slaves to righteous living. Because of the weakness of your human nature, I am using the illustration of slavery to help you understand all this. Previously, you let yourselves be slaves to impurity and lawlessness, which led ever deeper into sin. Now you must give yourselves to be slaves to righteous living so that you will become holy. (Romans 6: 16-19 NLT)*

Day 8

AT THE CROSS

I am
Blessed

Blessed be the God and Father of our Lord Jesus Christ,
who has blessed us with every spiritual blessing
in the heavenly places in Christ.
Ephesians 1:3

The flipside of being redeemed from the curse of the law is that you are blessed. I trust it is now firmly established in your heart that the divine exchange of the Cross involved Jesus becoming a curse so that you could be blessed.

Let's look at Galatians 3:13, which give us the full picture of the exchange.

> "Christ has redeemed us from the curse of the
> law, having become a curse for us (for it is written,
> "Cursed is everyone who hangs on a tree"), that the
> blessing of Abraham might come upon the Gentiles
> in Christ Jesus, that we might receive the promise
> of the Spirit through faith."

By putting your faith in the finished work of the Cross you are positioned in Christ, and being in Christ means that everything God blessed Abraham with is yours.

> *"So then those who are of faith are blessed with faithful Abraham... And if you are Christ's, then you are Abraham's seed, and heirs according to the promise." (Galatians 3:9, 29)*

The ultimate blessing of Abraham is the blessing of being made righteous by faith (Romans 4:13). By faith in Christ Jesus, we also receive the blessing of righteousness (2 Corinthians 5:21). According to today's key verse, God *"...has blessed us with **every** spiritual blessing in the heavenly places in Christ."* Every blessing you could ever desire has been given to you in Christ. Always remember the exchange! And don't think that because Ephesians 1:3 refers to "spiritual" blessing that tangible blessings such as good health and prosperity are not included—they are!

Today you may have a health or financial need, but if Jesus took every curse in His body, then surely you are now blessed with divine health and prosperity. So, believe and pronounce yourself blessed. All the blessings that were upon Jesus' life became yours when He traded places with you on the Cross and became a curse for you. They are spiritual blessings because they originate in the supernatural realm in God and flow into our lives by His Spirit. This is how Proverbs 10:22 in the Amplified translation describes this kind of blessing. *"The blessing of the Lord—it makes [truly] rich, and He adds no sorrow with it [neither does toiling increase it]."*

You will appreciate the magnitude of the blessing you have through the blood of Jesus when you consider the blessings that the blood of an animal brought the Children of Israel on the night of their deliverance from Egypt. God instructed them to apply the blood of the slain animal to their houses and pledged that when He sees the blood He will pass over them (Exodus 12:13).

With the blood on their houses, the Children of Israel were protected from the slaying of all firstborn in Egypt. Not only did God keep them safe through the blood, He also brought them forth with silver, gold, and in good health (Psalm 105:37).

Now, if the blood of an animal brought such blessing upon the people, how much more the Blood of our true Passover Lamb, Christ Jesus! It is significant to note that, through the pouring out of His Blood on the Cross, Jesus established a new covenant with God on our behalf. The blessings of the Cross are new covenant blessings (Matthew 26:28). As it was for Abraham, the new covenant blessings of the Blood of the Cross are for you and your descendants. It is the mercy of God and we thank Him for His bountiful blessing that extends to the generations.

> "As for Me, says the LORD, this is My covenant with them: My Spirit who is upon you, and My words which I have put in your mouth, shall not depart from your mouth, nor from the mouth of your descendants, nor from the mouth of your descendants' descendants, says the LORD, from this time and forevermore." put your faith in the blood of Jesus and believe for heaven's blessings to manifest in your life." (Isaiah 59:21)

The question of obedience often arises as a condition for receiving the blessing. Again, it is important to remember that when you are in Christ all that He is becomes yours, including His perfect obedience. While you cannot live in willful disobedience to God and expect His blessing to flow in your life, remember that you receive the blessing not by your merit, effort, or performance. You are blessed because of what Jesus has accomplished on your behalf.

Under the old covenant, the blessing was conditional on obedience, but mankind failed again and again. At the Cross, Jesus not only mediated a new covenant on our behalf, He also fulfilled its requirements. Let it be settled in your heart today that because of the Cross, you need not live another day apart from the blessing of God.

PERSONAL APPLICATION

Based on the divine exchange of the Cross, what blessing do you need to receive that is already yours in Christ?

_____

_____

_____

_____

_____

_____

_____

FAITH CONFESSION

I am blessed in every area of my life because through the finished work of the Cross I share in all the blessings of Christ Jesus.

PRAYER

Heavenly Father, thank you for your blessings that are upon my life. Help me to always remember that it is by faith in the finished work of Jesus that I receive your blessing, and not through self-effort. With your help, I will live with the consciousness that I am blessed so that my life can attract your blessings. Thank you for the assurance that your blessings are not only for me, but for my physical and spiritual descendants as well. Amen.

A DEEPER LOOK THROUGH THE WINDOW OF TRUTH

- *Blessings are on the head of the righteous. (Proverbs 10:6a)*
- *Blessed is the man who trusts in the LORD, and whose hope is the LORD. For he shall be like a tree planted by the waters, which spreads out its roots by the river, and will not fear when heat comes; but its leaf will be green, and will not be anxious in the year of drought, nor will cease from yielding fruit. (Jeremiah 17:7-8)*
- *By his divine power, God has given us everything we need for living a godly life. We have received all of this by coming to know him, the one who called us to himself by means of his marvelous glory and excellence. And because of his glory and excellence, he has given us great and precious promises. These are the promises that enable you to share his divine nature and escape the world's corruption caused by human desires. (2 Peter 1: 3-4 NLT)*

Day 9

AT THE CROSS

I am

Born Anew

Therefore, if anyone is in Christ, he is a new creation;
old things have passed away; behold, all things have become new.
2 Corinthians 5:17

One of the biggest mistakes we make is to think about our lives in one dimension only—the physical. Since our physical existence began with our parents, we have taken conception and birth as the beginning of our lives. Most individuals also think of their existence from the point of view of their physical bodies only without regard for the non-physical dimensions.

However, to fully appreciate what Jesus accomplished through the Cross, it is important to know that before you were conceived in your mother's womb your life began as a spirit being in God.

The record of Adam's creation as a spirit being after God's image in the first chapter of Genesis included you and me.

"Then God said, Let us make mankind in our image, in our likeness...

46

*So God created mankind in his own image, in the
image of God he created them; male and female
he created them." (Genesis 1:26-27 NIV)*

Likewise, Adam's sin and the resulting spiritual death (or
separation from God) also included us (Romans 5:12). But
through the Cross, Jesus Christ, the Last Adam, finished the
work that was necessary for you, me, and the entire human
race to be brought out of spiritual death.

*"For as in Adam all die, even so in Christ all shall
be made alive." (1 Corinthians 15:22)*

So what does the Cross mean to you? In light of what
you have just read, the Cross represents the one and only
opportunity for mankind to escape spiritual death and receive
new spiritual birth. That is what Jesus was talking about to
the man named Nichodemus in the Book of John when he
said, *"you must be born again."* Nichodemus, however, with
his one dimensional thinking, wondered how he could enter
his mother's womb a second time. Jesus then explained the
mystery: *"Flesh gives birth to flesh, but the Spirit gives birth to
spirit."* (See John 3:1-20)

This new birth comes about through the power of the
Cross. When you believe in your heart that Jesus died on
the Cross for your sins and was raised from the dead by the
Father, you receive God's free gift of eternal life and a reborn
spirit. That is the promise of John 3:16.

*"For God so loved the world that He gave His only
begotten Son, that whoever believes in Him should
not perish but have everlasting life."*

You may have been taught that you receive everlasting or eternal life only in heaven after you die. My friend, eternal life is not only about the future. It is the God-kind of life that you receive here and now in your reborn spirit, when you put your trust in the perfect sacrificial death of Jesus on the Cross. This is the ultimate meaning of the Cross.

According to 2 Corinthians 5:17, when we receive Christ we become a new creation or a new creature in Him. Outwardly there may be little or no change, but you can rest assured that in the innermost part of your being, in your spirit, you are made brand new with the life and nature of God.

My prayer for you today is that you would receive the revelation that through Jesus Christ, His shed Blood and finished work of the Cross, you are not only forgiven of your sins, but you have become a new person in Christ, totally free from your past. Like a newborn baby, your reborn spirit does not have a past. How liberating is that?

Let me ask you, what sin or painful memories have you been struggling with; divorce, adultery, molestation, immorality, perversion? Whatever it may be, you can settle it right now that in your spirit that is born anew in Christ, old things are passed away and ALL things are become new.

You need not live another day in bondage to your past. Focus on the life of God in your reborn spirit, and let the force of His divine life transform your body and soul. And remember, the sins you may commit in the future are already forgiven! The seed of God's life in you will not permit you to continue in wilful sin. But when you do miss the mark, repent quickly, confess the sin and receive the cleansing that is yours in the blood of Jesus (See 1 John 1:9).

My friend, it doesn't get any better than this: At the Cross new life is given!

If you have not yet received new life in Christ, this is your moment. May I invite you to pray these words from your heart so you can start afresh with a reborn spirit filled with God's life. Let's pray! *"I believe in my heart that Jesus died for my sins and was raised from the dead to give me new life. I now receive Jesus as my Lord and Savior."*

Congratulations! You're now a new creation in Christ!

PERSONAL APPLICATION

What misconceptions do you need to exchange at the Cross today to experience the new creation life in Christ?

_____

_____

_____

_____

_____

_____

_____

FAITH CONFESSION

I am a new creation in Christ Jesus. Outwardly I may appear the same, but inwardly I have been recreated in the image of my Father, God. I have a brand new beginning without the guilt, shame, and condemnation of the past.

PRAYER

Heavenly Father, thank you for the Cross! Thank you for the faith to believe and receive your gift of eternal life through Christ Jesus. Father, I rejoice to know that when you look at my inner man, my spirit, you see me perfect in Christ. Help me to see myself the way you see me and to think about myself the way you do. I ask you to give me the desire to read the Bible and feed on your Word, which is like milk to a newborn babe. I believe with all of my heart that by the power of your Word working in me I will be transformed into the person you created me to be, and fulfill your purpose for my life. Amen.

A DEEPER LOOK THROUGH THE WINDOW OF TRUTH

- *But to all who believed him and accepted him, he gave the right to become children of God. They are reborn—not with a physical birth resulting from human passion or plan, but a birth that comes from God. (1 John 1:12-13 NLT)*
- *For you have been born again, but not to a life that will quickly end. Your new life will last forever because it comes from the eternal, living word of God. (1 Peter 1:23 NLT)*
- *No one born (begotten) of God [deliberately, knowingly, and habitually] practices sin, for God's nature abides in him [His principle of life, the divine sperm, remains permanently within him]; and he cannot practice sinning because he is born (begotten) of God. (1 John 3:9 AMP)*
- *Yes, Adam's one sin brings condemnation for everyone, but Christ's one act of righteousness brings a right relationship with God and new life for everyone. (Romans 5:18 NLT)*
- *As newborn babes, desire the pure milk of the word, that you may grow thereby. (1 Peter 2:2)*

Day 10

I am

Righteous

For He made Him who knew no sin to be sin for us,
that we might become the righteousness of God in Him.
2 Corinthians 5:21

As a new creation in Christ it means that the perfect righteousness of Jesus Christ is now yours! The sin of the first Adam had brought the pronouncement of "none righteous" upon the entire human race. (Romans 3:10) Now, the Cross of the Last Adam, Jesus, has made us righteous. We are the beneficiary of an amazing divine exchange—Jesus became our sin and we became His righteousness. What a marvelous gift!

In Matthew 6:33 Jesus releases this instruction in what is commonly known as His Sermon on the Mount:

> *"But seek first the kingdom of God and His righteous-*
> *ness, and all these things shall be added to you."*

With these words, Jesus not only reveals the secret to

having our needs met, but also introduces a phenomenal shift in the standard by which we attain right relationship with God. Up to that time the Jews relied upon their own ability to keep the Law which God had given to Moses. Jesus came to fulfill the Law and the Prophets and to shift the people's perspective from law to grace.

> *"Don't misunderstand why I have come. I did not come to abolish the law of Moses or the writings of the prophets. No, I came to accomplish their purpose." (Matthew 5:17 NLT)*

> *"For the law was given through Moses, but grace and truth came through Jesus Christ." (John 1:17)*

The Cross is the absolute dividing line and altar of an unmistakable exchange. Because Jesus became sin on the Cross, you and I can receive God's gift of righteousness, not by any merit of our own, but solely on the merit of what Jesus has done. That's the power of the Cross!

As of today, let it be deeply impressed upon your heart that through the Cross you have received a righteousness that is based on Jesus' finished work, not your own works. Once you are in Christ you have His righteousness and you are righteous. Your righteousness is a state of being, not the result of the things you do.

With this understanding, we can see what Jesus was getting at in Matthew 6:33. The question remains, however, as many have asked—how does one seek God's righteousness? There are three steps:

First, accept by faith Jesus' perfect sacrifice at the Cross for your sin. You must believe that God raised Him from the dead as the life-giving Spirit by which you are born anew.

Second, acknowledge that God's righteousness is the person Jesus Christ, and believe that God sees you covered in His righteousness when you put your faith in His blood and sacrificial death.

Third, fix your mind on Jesus, your righteousness, rather than on your sins. You want the consciousness of who you are in Him to dominate your thoughts, because we always gravitate towards the object of our focus.

As the nature of Jesus becomes formed in you, so does His righteousness. This is the process by which you become established in righteousness and reap its rewards.

> *"In righteousness you will be established: Tyranny will be far from you; you will have nothing to fear. Terror will be far removed; it will not come near you." (Isaiah 54:14 NIV)*

Jesus promised that when we seek His righteousness all things will be added. Did you notice the "additions" in this verse? Freedom from oppression, fear and terror. The amazing thing about the righteousness which is by faith is that it works on our behalf. We get to rest from our works and enjoy its fruit and effects.

> *"The fruit of that righteousness will be peace; its effect will be quietness and confidence forever." (Isaiah 32:17 NIV)*

Let the righteousness you have received at the Cross now attract and add all the blessings that God has always intended for you.

PERSONAL APPLICATION

What misconceptions do you need to exchange at the Cross today to enjoy God's gift of righteousness?

_____

_____

_____

_____

_____

_____

_____

_____

FAITH CONFESSION

I am righteous because at the Cross Jesus took my sin and gave me His righteousness. My righteousness is of faith.

PRAYER

Heavenly Father, thank you for transferring the righteousness of Jesus to me because of His shed blood and perfect sacrifice at the Cross. According to your Word, Father, I believe that all your blessings will begin to flow into my life as I seek to have Jesus and His righteousness established in my heart above all else. I ask you to remove every obstacle to the expression of my gift of righteousness. Amen.

A Deeper Look Through the Window of Truth

- *But people are counted as righteous, not because of their work, but because of their faith in God who forgives sinners. (Romans 4:5 NLT)*
- *For if, by the trespass of the one man, death reigned through that one man, how much more will those who receive God's abundant provision of grace and of the gift of righteousness reign in life through the one man, Jesus Christ! (Romans 5:17 NIV)*
- *I do not treat the grace of God as meaningless. For if keeping the law could make us right with God, then there was no need for Christ to die. (Galatians 2:21 NLT)*
- *Throw off your old sinful nature and your former way of life, which is corrupted by lust and deception. Instead, let the Spirit renew your thoughts and attitudes. Put on your new nature, created to be like God—truly righteous and holy. (Ephesians 4:22-24 NLT)*
- *For You, O LORD, will bless the righteous; With favor You will surround him as with a shield. (Psalm 5:12)*

Day 11

AT THE CROSS

I am
Fathered

*Jesus said to her, "... Go to My brethren and say to them,
'I am ascending to My Father and your Father,
and to My God and your God."'*
John 20:17

As we pass over the half way point of our journey of discovery, I trust that the meaning of the Cross is becoming increasingly clear to you.

Today's key verse pinpoints the one thing that I believe was foremost in Jesus' heart as He endured the suffering and death of the Cross. The recorded words of John 20:17 were spoken by Jesus to Mary Magdalene as she stood outside the empty tomb on the morning of His resurrection.

It is very significant that these first words were a commission and a message concerning the shared Fatherhood connection between Jesus and His disciples: *"Go to my brethren and say to them, 'I am ascending to My Father and your Father.'"* Jesus had previously introduced the concept of a shared relationship with

God as Father when He instructed His disciples to pray, "*Our Father.*" Now, on this side of the Cross He wanted them to know the relationship was now officially sealed—I am going to the one who is not only my Father and God, but yours as well.

You see, God's original intent in creation was to have a family of human offspring. He desired sons and daughters in relationship with Him and representing Him on the earth. Created in the image and likeness of God, Adam was more than just the first created man. His true identity according to Luke 3:38, was "*Adam, the son of God.*"

Restoring God's original intent and purpose for humanity is central to the meaning of the Cross. It is therefore important to recognize and appreciate that the new life you receive in Christ as a new creation is the Father's life. So, don't make the mistake of settling for a faith that is content with the initial salvation experience when there is so much more to your spiritual inheritance. The Cross gives you access to a lifetime of relationship with God as your Heavenly Father and getting to know Him better.

> "*I have not stopped giving thanks for you, remembering you in my prayers... I keep asking that the God of our Lord Jesus Christ, the glorious Father, may give you the Spirit of wisdom and revelation, so that you may know him better.*" (*Ephesians 1:16-17 NIV*)

Think for a moment what it means to have God as your Heavenly Father. You are born from His seed and you have His DNA! (1 John 3:9) Moreover, as your Heavenly Father you can be confident about God caring for your needs. (Matthew 6:8)

Growing deeper in a relationship with God as your Father is essential for you to develop a sense of identity, security and satisfaction. Philip requested of Jesus in John 14:8, *"Lord, show us the Father, and we will be satisfied."* My friend, you will find satisfaction and fulfillment in your Christian walk when you fully recognize that it is first and foremost about relationship, rather than rules to follow.

Through the Cross Jesus opens the door to your relationship with the Heavenly Father. (John 10:9; 14:6) It is the Holy Spirit who comes to live in you when you are born anew. He continues the work of revealing the Father to you and drawing you closer to Him.

It has been said that the greatest hunger in the world is not food hunger, but father hunger. This may very well be true because of the void left by absent and dysfunctional fathers. Well, the message of the Cross is good news for everyone, for at the Cross the hunger for a father's love and acceptance is fully satisfied. At the Cross, the imperfections of the natural father are swallowed up by the unfailing love of God the Perfect Father.

Your Heavenly Father's love for you is perfect, regardless of where you have been or what you have done. As Jesus had prayed to the Father in John 17, I pray that you would receive deep in your heart the truth that God your Father loves you with the same love He has for Jesus.

> *"That the world will know that you sent me and that you love them as much as you love me... Then your love for me will be in them, and I will be in them." (John 17:23b, 26bNLT)*

Meditate on this truth until you heart embraces it fully and you find your place in the loving arms of your Heavenly Father.

PERSONAL APPLICATION

What misconceptions about God as your Father do you need to exchange at the Cross?

_____

_____

_____

_____

_____

_____

_____

_____

FAITH CONFESSION

My Father in heaven loves me as He loves Jesus.

PRAYER

Heavenly Father, thank you for going to the extreme of the Cross to bring me back into relationship with you. Help me by your Holy Spirit to grow deeper in my fellowship with you so, I can know you better and become the person you created me to be. I ask you to daily pour your love into my heart and help me receive your love. I give you permission to remove every wrong concept I have about you as Father and fill me with the revelation of who you truly are. Amen.

A DEEPER LOOK THROUGH THE WINDOW OF TRUTH

- *"I thought to myself, 'I would love to treat you as my own children!' I wanted nothing more than to give you this beautiful land—the finest possession in the world. I looked*

> forward to your calling me 'Father,' and I wanted you never to turn from me. *(Jeremiah 3:19 NLT)*

- "I will be a Father to you, And you shall be My sons and daughters, Says the LORD Almighty." *(2 Corinthians 6:18)*
- And because you are sons, God has sent forth the Spirit of His Son into your hearts, crying out, "Abba, Father!" *(Galatians 4:6)*
- Behold what manner of love the Father has bestowed on us, that we should be called children of God! Therefore the world does not know us, because it did not know Him. *(I John 3:1)*

Day 12

AT THE CROSS

I find
Friendship

Greater love has no one than this,
than to lay down one's life for his friends.
John 15:13

**In chapter ten of the Gospel of John, Jesus identifies Himself as the Good Shepherd who lays down His life for the sheep. He then went on to say something very significant. *"No one can take my life from me. I sacrifice it voluntarily."* (John 10:18 NLT) When you connect this statement with today's key verse you see that Jesus' sacrificial death on the Cross represents the ultimate expression of true friendship.

Some find it hard to think in terms of friendship with God, considering it presumptuous. But we need not dismiss this aspect of the relationship God wants to have with us.

- God called Abraham His friend. (Isaiah 41:8; James 2:23)

- God spoke to Moses face-to-face as one speaks to a friend. (Exodus 33:11)
- Jesus says He no longer calls His followers servants, but friends. (John 15:15)

If prior to the Cross God called Abraham His friend, on this side of the Cross (where we possess the righteousness of faith through Jesus), we can be sure that we also have the privilege of sharing in this friendship relationship. Your faith in the finished work of the Cross puts you in Christ, makes you a seed of Abraham and positions you to receive the blessing of friendship that Abraham enjoyed with God. (Galatians 3:29)

Through my interaction with callers on the call-in television program, I am fully aware of the intense emotional pain that loneliness causes. Loneliness has reached epidemic proportions and no age group is immune. For younger generations the crisis is even more acute, because the internet culture of social media networks has forced upon them a false sense of relationship and friendship.

Where are you in relation to this epidemic? Is loneliness one of your greatest fears? Are you caught in the social media web, but still longing for true friendships? Are you finding it difficult to build lasting friendships?

Wherever you are, you need not go another day without recognizing and embracing the friendship you find through Jesus. At the Cross Jesus experienced desertion, rejection and loneliness, so that you might find acceptance and friendship. At the height of Jesus' suffering, Mark 14:50 says, "*They all forsook him and fled.*"

Well, you may say that this is all well and good, but what you need is friendship with a person who you can see face to face. God understands—He wired you for friendship and relationship. But here's the secret. When you fully embrace God's friendship through the Cross, a transformation will take place in you that makes you less needy and more "friendly."

Remember Matthew 16:33. *"But seek first the kingdom of God and His righteousness, and all these things shall be added to you."* Living with a consciousness of your belonging to God's Kingdom family and the gift of righteousness you receive at the Cross are the keys that will add friendships and every other thing you need in life.

PERSONAL APPLICATION

What misconceptions do you need to exchange at the Cross for friendships to grow in your life?

_____

_____

_____

_____

_____

_____

_____

_____

FAITH CONFESSION

I am a friend of God.

PRAYER

Heavenly Father, thank you for sending Jesus to the earth and for His willingness to lay down His life for me, so that I could be called a friend of God. Thank you, Father, that you know all about my weaknesses, yet you desire friendship with me. Help me to grow in my confidence that because you gave up your Son, Jesus, for me, you will meet my need for good friends. Amen.

A DEEPER LOOK THROUGH THE WINDOW OF TRUTH

- *For since our friendship with God was restored by the death of his Son while we were still his enemies, we will certainly be saved through the life of his Son. So now we can rejoice in our wonderful new relationship with God because our Lord Jesus Christ has made us friends of God. (Romans 5:10-11 NLT)*
- *The LORD is a friend to those who fear him. He teaches them his covenant. (Psalm 25:14 NLT)*
- *A man who has friends must himself be friendly, But there is a friend who sticks closer than a brother. (Proverbs 18:24)*
- *"If you love me, show it by doing what I've told you. I will talk to the Father, and he'll provide you another Friend so that you will always have someone with you. This Friend is the Spirit of Truth. The godless world can't take him in because it doesn't have eyes to see him, doesn't know what to look for. But you know him already because he has been staying with you, and will even be in you! (John 14:15-17 MSG)*

Day 13

AT THE CROSS

I receive

Peace

Peace I leave with you, My peace I give to you;
not as the world gives do I give to you.
Let not your heart be troubled, neither let it be afraid.
John 14:27

Troubled hearts. Fearful hearts. For one reason or another, these conditions seem to abound everywhere, even among believers in Christ. Day after day, increasing threat of diseases, terrorism, economic collapse, nations at war, family and personal crises of all sorts rob our peace. The words of Jesus in Luke 21:26 fittingly describe our times: *"Men's hearts failing them from fear and the expectations of those things which are coming on the earth."*

But take heart, my friend! If you need peace, today is your day to know Jesus not only as Savior, but also as your Prince of Peace (Isaiah 9:6). Today is your day to receive the gift of eternal, abiding peace that is available to you only through Jesus Christ and the finished work of His Cross.

We lost both peace *with* God and the peace *of* God through Adam's sin and since then humanity has been on a desperate quest to compensate for the loss. Sadly, some have said that even after receiving Jesus Christ as Savior they still don't have peace. Jesus came to seek and to save *"that which was lost"* (Luke 19:10), and through the blood of the Cross God has reconciled all things to Himself. (Colossians 1:20) The way has certainly been made through the Cross for you to receive peace.

> *"Therefore, since we have been made right in God's sight by faith, we have **peace with God** because of what Jesus Christ our Lord has done for us."* *(Romans 5:1 NLT)*

If you have found peace *with* God through the Lord Jesus, but have not been experiencing the peace *of* God, you are not alone. I often speak to individuals on the weekly call-in television program who are seeking freedom from the turmoil, uncertainty, pain, loss or fear caused by some kind of financial, health, emotional, family or other issue. They are crying out for peace of mind.

Peace of mind is a wonderful thing, but when it is dependent on circumstances and happenings it is at best temporary, incomplete and fragile. But the peace you receive through Jesus' finished work of the Cross is the opposite and that's the kind of peace you really want. The peace of the Cross is enduring, because it is an expression of God's loving-kindness, which produces complete wholeness and well-being. This is what the Hebrew word *"shalom"* represents—complete peace which brings your whole life into divine order.

So, how do we lay hold of this peace? There are four ways: First, by revelation of the Spirit, which enables you to recognize and live with a consciousness of all that Jesus went through to exchange your enmity with God and personal turmoil for His perfect peace. *"The chastisement [needful to obtain] peace and well-being for us was upon Him."* *(Isaiah 53:5 AMP)*

Second, by believing that you have peace as a result of your righteousness in Christ. *"And the effect of righteousness will be peace [internal and external]."* *(Isaiah 32:17 AMP)*

Third, by nurturing your relationship with Jesus as your Prince of Peace and the ultimate source of your peace. As you keep your mind fixed on Jesus (Isaiah 26:3), then even in a raging storm you will hear Him speak into your circumstances, *"Peace, be still!"* *(Mark 4:39)*

Fourth, by choosing the path of prayer and thanksgiving over worry and anxiety. *"Be anxious for nothing, but in everything by prayer and supplication, with thanksgiving, let your requests be made known to God; and the **peace of God**, which surpasses all understanding, will guard your hearts and minds through Christ Jesus."* *(Philippians 4:6-7)*

Don't live another day without the peace that Jesus bequeathed to you through the Cross—His own peace! It is a complete package that restores you to peace with God, gives you the peace of God in trying circumstances, enabling you to be at peace with yourself and to live at peace with others.

Now, a command from the Apostle Paul from Colossians 3:15: *"Let the peace of God rule in your heart!"*

PERSONAL APPLICATION

What do you need to exchange at the Cross today to possess peace that is not affected by your circumstances?

_____

_____

_____

_____

_____

_____

_____

FAITH CONFESSION

The Prince of Peace lives in me and His abiding peace rules in my heart.

PRAYER

Heavenly Father, I thank you that through Jesus Christ and the blood of His Cross you have given me your enduring peace. Because I now have both the peace of God and peace with God, I need not fear the turmoil around me or the uncertainties of life. I ask you, Father, to establish me in your peace so that I can experience the blessing of complete wholeness and well being in all areas of my life. Amen.

A DEEPER LOOK THROUGH THE WINDOW OF TRUTH

- *But now in Christ Jesus you who once were far off have been brought near by the blood of Christ. For He Himself is our peace, who has made both one, and has broken down the middle wall of separation. (Ephesians 2:13-14)*

- *And through him God reconciled everything to himself. He made peace with everything in heaven and on earth by means of Christ's blood on the cross. (Colossians 1:20 NLT)*
- *Through the tender mercy of our God, with which the Dayspring from on high has visited us; to give light to those who sit in darkness and the shadow of death, to guide our feet into the way of peace. (Luke 1:78-79)*
- *For the mountains shall depart and the hills be removed, But My kindness shall not depart from you, nor shall My covenant of peace be removed," Says the LORD, who has mercy on you. (Isaiah 54:10)*
- *I will make peace your leader and righteousness your ruler. (Isaiah 60:17b)*
- *The LORD will give strength to His people; the LORD will bless His people with peace. (Psalm 29:11)*

Day 14

AT THE CROSS

I find

Prosperity

For you know the grace of our Lord Jesus Christ,
that though He was rich, yet for your sakes He became
poor, that you through His poverty might become rich.
2 Corinthians 8:9

Your focus at the Cross yesterday was on finding peace. Today we continue on the same path with an emphasis on prosperity. The Hebrew word for peace from yesterday's reading, *shalom*, also encompasses your prosperity. So having the peace *of* God and peace *with* God translates to prosperity.

Look at today's key verse again: "*For you know the grace of our Lord Jesus Christ, that though He was rich, yet for your sakes He became poor, that you through His poverty might become rich.*" What an amazing divine exchange! Jesus traded places with you. He took your poverty and gave you His riches—His superabundance! That's the prosperity you find at the Cross.

Now, what does this superabundance include? Well, it certainly includes material wealth and so much more. 3 John

2 captures the comprehensiveness of the prosperity that God desires for you.

> *"Beloved, I pray that in all respects you may prosper and be in good health, just as your soul prospers." (NASB)*

The little phrase *"all respects"* means what it says. So, if you are presently experiencing lack in any area of your life, know that God has provided for your prosperity through the Cross and in Jesus. That is the promise of Philippians 4:19: *"And my God will liberally supply (fill to the full) your every need according to His riches in glory in Christ Jesus." (AMP)*

God prospered Abraham in all things and it is for you too as an offspring of Abraham by faith. (Genesis 24:1; Galatians 3:29) The question often arises: How do we experience the fulfillment of God's promise in our day-to-day lives? I believe the secret is in the last phrase of 3 John 2, *"... just as your soul prospers."*

The riches of Christ Jesus (wisdom and creative ability) to help us prosper were deposited in your spirit when you were born again as a new creation. However, for the riches of your spirit to become your reality you soul (mind, emotions and will) must cooperate with your spirit.

The Bible describes this process as the restoring of your soul and the renewing of your mind. (Psalm 23:3; Romans 12:2) Your thoughts and words originate in your soul and shape your reality. One of the keys to your prosperity then is to ensure that your thoughts about yourself reflect the Word of God. You become what you think and that's why the Bible says, *"As a man thinks in his heart so is he." (Proverbs 23:7 KJV)* Prosper in your soul and you will see prosperity in other areas of your life.

One final and crucial thought from the life of a man in the Old Testament named Job, whom the Bible said was a righteous man. Job experienced a severe attack from satan in which he lost everything except his life. In the end, God prospered Job with a double portion of all he had lost. But here is the critical point. At God's instruction, Job had to first pray for, forgive, and release his three so called friends whose judgments about Job's situation had really hurt him.

Job obeyed God instructions and God prospered him. *"After Job prayed for his friends, the LORD restored Job's prosperity and gave him twice as much as he had before." (Job 42:10 GW)*

For us on this side of the Cross, our prosperity is already restored in Christ. May you by God's grace attend to the health of your soul and exercise your faith to receive all that God has for you.

PERSONAL APPLICATION

What do you need to exchange at the Cross today to prosper in areas where you may presently be experiencing lack?

FAITH CONFESSION

Through the riches of Christ, God's abundant supply is available to me in all areas of my life.

PRAYER

Heavenly Father, thank you that your desire is for me to prosper in all areas of my life. Thank you for making this possible through the Cross. I ask you to remove from my soul anything such as unforgiveness, wrong beliefs and fear that would limit my capacity to experience your prosperity. Help me by your grace to live with a greater consciousness of your abundance than of the present needs in my life. Amen.

A DEEPER LOOK THROUGH THE WINDOW OF TRUTH

- *And you shall remember the LORD your God, for it is He who gives you power to get wealth, that He may establish His covenant which He swore to your fathers, as it is this day. (Deuteronomy 8:18)*
- *This Book of the Law shall not depart from your mouth, but you shall meditate in it day and night, that you may observe to do according to all that is written in it. For then you will make your way prosperous, and then you will have good success. (Joshua 1:8)*
- *And God is able to bless you abundantly, so that in all things at all times, having all that you need, you will abound in every good work.... You will be enriched in every way so that you can be generous on every occasion, and through us your generosity will result in thanksgiving to God. (2 Corinthians 9:8, 11 NIV)*

- *Finally, brethren, whatever things are true, whatever things are noble, whatever things are just, whatever things are pure, whatever things are lovely, whatever things are of good report, if there is any virtue and if there is anything praiseworthy—meditate on these things. (Philippians 4:8)*
- *And do not be conformed to this world, but be transformed by the renewing of your mind, that you may prove what is that good and acceptable and perfect will of God. (Romans 12:2)*

Day 15

AT THE CROSS

I am
Healed

*But he was pierced for our transgressions,
he was crushed for our iniquities; the punishment that
brought us peace was on him, and by his wounds we are healed.*
Isaiah 53:5 NIV

Let me remind you of something you read on Day 7: *When
you put your faith in the finished work of the Cross, you experience
the divine exchange that Jesus accomplished on your behalf. The
blessing instead of the curse...For sickness He has given you health.*

You find health at the Cross because with every stroke
of beating, every crushing blow, every tearing of His flesh and
with each piercing, Jesus took the pain and affliction of your
sickness upon His body. But that's not all. With every ounce
of blood that flowed from His wounds, Jesus broke the curse
of sickness, disease and infirmity over your life and paid for
your healing.

I have discovered that some folks find it easier to believe
for forgiveness of sins through the Cross than to believe for

75

healing from sickness and disease. But, the Word of God does not lie and Isaiah 53:4-5 clearly describes double cure of the Cross—forgiveness and healing. The Amplified Translation of these verses drive home the point.

> "Surely He has borne our griefs (sicknesses, weaknesses, and distresses) and carried our sorrows and pains [of punishment], yet we [ignorantly] considered Him stricken, smitten, and afflicted by God [as if with leprosy]. But He was wounded for our transgressions, He was bruised for our guilt and iniquities; the chastisement [needful to obtain] peace and well-being for us was upon Him, and with the stripes [that wounded] Him we are healed and made whole."

If you are presently battling an illness, you may be wondering how to apply this Word to activate healing in your body. First, it is important for you to know and believe wholeheartedly that God wants you to live in health. Sickness is not from God and contrary to what you may have heard, God does not use sickness to punish His children or teach them anything.

Now, let me share some practical insights with you.

1. Do not wait until you have a health issue to start believing and claiming the healing that Jesus purchased for you at the Cross. Even when you are in good health, ward off sickness and disease each day by speaking in faith what the Word of God says about your healing—sickness and disease has no power over you because you are healed of the Lord.
2. Focus on the health of your soul life. You will remember from yesterday's reading that your prosperity and

health are directly linked to the prosperity of your soul. "*Beloved, I pray that in all respects you may prosper and be in good health, just as your soul prospers.*" *(3 John 2 NASB)* Keeping your heart and mind free from bitterness, unforgiveness, envy, toxic thoughts and negative attitudes will promote good health.

3. Watch your words. The words we speak eventually manifest as our physical reality. If you are seeking the Lord for healing, then thank Him for healing you before it happens. Listen to what Proverbs 18:21 says in the Good News Translation. "*What you say can preserve life or destroy it; so you must accept the consequences of your words.*" Proverbs 12:18b also says that the tongue of the wise brings healing.

4. Eat the bread of healing. Each time you take the Holy Communion, eat the bread with a consciousness that it represents the body of Jesus that was broken for your health. Take the bread as a point of contact to activate your faith to receive the healing that is already yours (see Matthew 26:26; Luke 22:19).

The manifestation of healing is often gradual, so I encourage you to persevere with your focus firmly fixed on the finished work of the Cross and your trust anchored in God's healing power.

PERSONAL APPLICATION

What do you need to exchange at the Cross today to come into agreement with what God's Word says about your healing?

_____

_____

_____

_____

_____

_____

_____

FAITH CONFESSION

Jesus took my sicknesses in His body, paid for my healing with His blood, and by His wounds I am healed.

PRAYER

Heavenly Father, thank you for not only forgiving all my sins, but also healing all my diseases through the Blood and broken body of Jesus. Help me to believe with all of my heart that your desire is for me to live in divine health. Help me to receive and speak your Word, which is medicine to my whole body. Amen

A DEEPER LOOK THROUGH THE WINDOW OF TRUTH

- *Who Himself bore our sins in His own body on the tree, that we, having died to sins, might live for righteousness—by whose stripes you were healed. (1 Peter 2:24)*

- *By faith in the name of Jesus, this man whom you see and know was made strong. It is Jesus' name and the faith that comes through him that has completely healed him, as you can all see. (Acts 3:16 NIV)*
- *Praise the LORD, my soul; all my inmost being, praise his holy name. Praise the LORD, my soul, and forget not all his benefits—who forgives all your sins and heals all your diseases. (Psalm 103:1-3 NIV)*
- *And the LORD will take away from you all sickness, and will afflict you with none of the terrible diseases of Egypt which you have known, but will lay them on all those who hate you. (Deuteronomy 7:15)*
- *Heal me, O LORD, and I shall be healed; Save me, and I shall be saved, For You are my praise. Indeed they say to me, "Where is the word of the LORD? Let it come now!" (Jeremiah 17:14-15)*
- *For I will restore health to you and heal you of your wounds," says the LORD. (Jeremiah 30:17a)*

Day 16

AT THE CROSS

I find

Protection

*Now the blood shall be a sign for you on the
houses where you are. And when I see the blood,
I will pass over you; and the plague shall not be on you
to destroy you when I strike the land of Egypt.*
Exodus 12:13

The protection you find at the Cross is through the covering of the Blood of Jesus. Today's good news is that because of your relationship with Jesus you need not fear the calamity, disasters, epidemics, diseases and sudden destruction of our times. The precious Blood of Jesus is your protection and covering.

You may recognize that the context of today's key verse is God's provision for the protection of the Children of Israel when death swept through the land of Egypt. God's final judgment against Pharaoh for his refusal to let God's people go was the death of every Egyptian first born. The Children of Israel were untouched, however, because they obeyed God's instruction to kill a spotless lamb and apply its blood over the doors of their homes.

At the Cross, Jesus was slain as your Passover Lamb and His blood is available as your defense and for your full protection. Today is your day to believe in the power of the blood of Jesus and bring your life and your entire household under its protective power.

How do we do that? We apply the protection of the Blood of Jesus through prayer, by speaking God's Word and by declaring that our lives and all that pertains to us are covered by the Blood. This is done, of course, in the realm of faith and by the power of the Holy Spirit who is one with the Blood of Jesus and makes it continually effective. *"And there are three that bear witness on earth: the Spirit, the water, and the blood; and these three agree as one." (I John 5:8)*

Psalm 91 is one of the Bible passages most read for protection. However, it is faith in the finished work of the Cross that releases the protection that the Psalm promises. The Blood of Jesus renders evil forces powerless. The eternal Blood of Jesus defeated satan at the Cross and remains eternally effective against him and his works.

God has certainly done His part in making provision for our protection. Now we have a part to play. We must resist fear because fear breaks down the protective hedge that God has afforded us through the finished work of the Cross.

There are to two specific dimensions of the protection that is yours through the Cross:

1. The covering of Jesus' robe of righteousness. Putting your faith in the finished work of the Cross is putting on the robe of righteousness that Jesus purchased for you with His blood. In the righteousness of

Jesus is everything you need, including God's seal of protection. *"I will greatly rejoice in the LORD, My soul shall be joyful in my God; for He has clothed me with the garments of salvation, He has covered me with the robe of righteousness." (Isaiah 61:10)*

2. The covering of the love of God. The love of God is an unbeatable force. God's love is the reason for your existence and is also the reason for the Cross. The love that God demonstrated towards you in giving Jesus as a sacrifice for your sin is the same love that provides you with divine protection. *"He who did not spare His own Son, but delivered Him up for us all, how shall He not with Him also freely give us all things?... For I am persuaded that neither death nor life, nor angels nor principalities nor powers, nor things present nor things to come, nor height nor depth, nor any other created thing, shall be able to separate us from the love of God which is in Christ Jesus our Lord." (Romans 8:32, 38-39)*

You also have the protection of the full armor of God that enables you to stand against attacks from satan's kingdom. I encourage you to read Ephesians 6:10-18. It will familiarize you with the parts of your spiritual armor of protection.

Remember that prayer is the primary strategy by which you activate the protection that God has afforded you through the Blood and Cross of Jesus Christ. God has done His part. Now it's up to you to do your part. My prayer is that with a heart full of faith you will be diligent in activating the protection of the Cross over yourself and your family.

PERSONAL APPLICATION

What do you need to exchange at the Cross to experience its protective power?

_____

_____

_____

_____

_____

_____

_____

_____

FAITH CONFESSION

Destruction shall not come near me or my household, because we are protected by the blood of Jesus, our Passover Lamb.

PRAYER

Heavenly Father, thank you for the gift of Jesus as my Passover Lamb and for the protection of His precious Blood. As I release my faith in prayer today, I activate the protection of the Blood of Jesus, the protection of His righteousness and the protection that the covering of your unfailing love provides. Help me to resist fear at all times so that I can rest in the peace of your protection that is available to me at the Cross. Amen.

A DEEPER LOOK THROUGH THE WINDOW OF TRUTH

- *For the LORD will pass through the land to strike down the Egyptians. But when he sees the blood on the top and sides*

> *of the doorframe, the LORD will pass over your home. He will not permit his death angel to enter your house and strike you down. (Exodus 12:23 NLT)*

- *The LORD is my light and my salvation; whom shall I fear? The LORD is the strength of my life; of whom shall I be afraid? When the wicked came against me to eat up my flesh, my enemies and foes, they stumbled and fell. Though an army may encamp against me, my heart shall not fear; though war may rise against me, in this I will be confident. (Psalm 27:1-3)*
- *I will both lie down in peace, and sleep; for You alone, O LORD, make me dwell in safety. (Psalm 4:8)*
- *For the angel of the LORD is a guard; he surrounds and defends all who fear him. (Psalm 34:7 NLT)*

Day 17

AT THE CROSS

I find

Security

*The fruit of righteousness will be peace, and the outcome
of righteousness, calm and security forever.*
Isaiah 32:17 CEB

What the world offers as security is at best temporary and vulnerable. I don't know about you, but that is not good enough for me. I want a "forever security." Today's key verse points us to the source: *"The outcome of righteousness is calm and security forever."* Praise God!

From Day 10 you understand that when you put your faith in Jesus and His finished work at the Cross, His righteousness is transferred to you. The righteousness of Jesus is eternal, unshakeable and unchanging—it is forever righteousness. Not only that; it bears fruit in your life: peace, calm and security that is not subject to the experiences and circumstances of life.

I want to draw your attention to another source of your security: The unfailing love of God for you, from which you can *never* be separated.

> *"Who shall separate us from the love of Christ? Shall tribulation, or distress, or persecution, or famine, or nakedness, or peril, or sword? ... For I am persuaded that neither nor life, nor angels nor principalities nor powers, nor things present nor things to come, nor height nor depth, nor any other created thing, shall be able to separate us from the love of God which is in Christ Jesus our Lord."* (Romans 8:35, 38-39)

Friend, that is the Word of God and you could not ask for a stronger assurance of security than that. Let me remind you that from the first day of this amazing journey of discovery you saw that the Cross was the ultimate expression of God's love for you. *"God demonstrates His own love toward us, in that while we were still sinners, Christ died for us." (Romans 5:8)*

You also have the promise of an internal inheritance (one that lasts forever), through the Blood of Jesus.

> *"Because Christ offered himself to God, he is able to bring a new promise from God. Through his death he paid the price to set people free from the sins they committed under the first promise. He did this so that those who are called can be guaranteed an inheritance that will last forever."* (Hebrews 9:15 GW)

That inheritance blessing is God's gift to you as one born anew in Christ and it is secure. Let us join the Apostle Peter in praising God for this secure eternal inheritance.

> *"Praise be to the God and Father of our Lord Jesus Christ! In his great mercy he has given us new birth*

into a living hope through the resurrection of Jesus Christ from the dead, and into an inheritance that can never perish, spoil or fade. This inheritance is kept in heaven for you, who through faith are shielded by God's power until the coming of the salvation that is ready to be revealed in the last time." (1 Peter 3:4-5 NIV)

The secret to experiencing the security of the Cross lies in your consciousness of who you are as God's beloved, as a new creation in Christ, and as one who is righteous in Christ. May you be one whose heart becomes securely established in the Rock Christ Jesus and all that He has accomplished for you at the Cross.

As we wrap up for today, let me share with you the awesome benefits of a secure heart.

"They will have no fear of bad news; their hearts are steadfast, trusting in the LORD. Their hearts are secure, they will have no fear; in the end they will look in triumph on their foes. They have freely scattered their gifts to the poor, their righteousness endures forever; their horn will be lifted high in honor." (Psalm 112:7-9 NIV)

PERSONAL APPLICATION

What do you need to exchange at the Cross today to develop a more secure heart?

_____

_____

_____

_____

_____

_____

FAITH CONFESSION

I am secure in Christ because nothing can separate me from the love God has for me.

PRAYER

Heavenly Father, thank you for the blessing of security that I receive at the Cross through the righteousness of Jesus. In the uncertainty of our changing world, your gift of security that I find at the Cross is a most valuable treasure. I ask you to pour your grace into my heart, so that I remain securely anchored in your unfailing love at all times. Amen.

A DEEPER LOOK THROUGH THE WINDOW OF TRUTH

- *And He will be the stability of your times, a wealth of salvation, wisdom and knowledge; The fear of the LORD is his treasure. (Isaiah 33:6 NASB)*

- *My people will dwell in a peaceful habitation, in secure dwellings, and in quiet resting places. (Isaiah 32:18)*
- *Return to the stronghold [of security and prosperity], you prisoners of hope; even today do I declare that I will restore double your former prosperity to you. (Zechariah 9:12 AMP)*
- *It is God who arms me with strength and keeps my way secure. (Psalm 18:32 NIV)*
- *Those who fear the LORD are secure; he will be a refuge for their children. (Proverbs 14:26 NIV)*

Day 18

AT THE CROSS

I find

Freedom

*Jesus, who offered himself in exchange for
everyone held captive by sin, to set them all free.*
1 Timothy 2:5b-6a

We embarked on this Twenty-One Day Journey for the express purpose of making the divine exchange of the Cross real to us personally in our day-to-day lives. With only a few days left, I want to commend you on your perseverance. Your labor is not in vain!

As you have been putting the Cross centre stage of your life every day, I pray that going forward you will know by experience the joy of freedom that is found only by going through the door of the Cross. As the Apostle Paul wrote in Galatians 1:5 GW, *"Christ has freed us so that we may enjoy the benefits of freedom. Therefore be firm in this freedom, and don't become slaves again."*

It is critical that we take heed to what this verse is saying and not give up the freedom that Jesus paid for with the high price of His precious Blood and Life. We must guard this freedom from God, for it is the key to experiencing the many benefits of the Cross that we have been exploring. This freedom is not a licence to do whatever we want, as this passage makes clear:

> *"So, since we're out from under the old tyranny, does that mean we can live any old way we want? Since we're free in the freedom of God, can we do anything that comes to mind? Hardly. You know well enough from your own experience that there are some acts of so-called freedom that destroy freedom. Offer yourselves to sin, for instance, and it's your last free act. But offer yourselves to the ways of God and the freedom never quits. All your lives you've let sin tell you what to do. But thank God you've started listening to a new master, one whose commands set you free to live openly in his freedom!" (Romans 6:15-18 MSG)*

I'd like to reinforce that last statement with John 8:36: *"Therefore if the Son makes you free, you shall be free indeed."*

The work that was necessary to set you free from the tyranny of sin has been completed at the Cross. It is finished! Now, how about the part you have to play to make this costly freedom your personal experience? Listen to what Matthew 6:15 says in The Message, *"If you refuse to do your part, you cut yourself off from God's part."*

I know you want to enjoy the benefits of the freedom Christ purchased for you and safeguard it as best you can. I also desire the same thing. So let's look at a few of the ways we can do our part, so that we are not cut off from God's part.

Know Truth: Let the truth of the finished work of

the Cross penetrate the depths of your heart and soul by meditating and thinking on what God has said about you and how He sees you in Christ. It is not just truth that sets you free, but the truth that you have taken hold of as your own. Jesus declared in John 8:32 NIV, *"Then you will know the truth, and the truth will set you free."* The number one truth for you to be conscious of at all times is that because you are righteous in Christ His righteousness controls all areas of your life.

Renew Your Mind: The experience of true freedom begins in your mind. Fill your mind with thoughts of the freedom that Jesus has purchased for you and the expressions of your life will begin to align with who you really are as a new creation in Christ

Know Why Jesus Set You Free: I believe that knowing the purpose for your freedom will motivate you to guard against losing it. You have been set free from bondage to sin to live out your God-given identity and destiny. With freedom in Christ it is now possible for you to become the person God created you to be.

Know How To Guard Your Freedom: Guarding your freedom is about being conscious of what you are yielding yourself to and the choices you are making. Choose the way of the Cross, rather than the way of self will. In this way, the Cross as the power of God will break the power of sin in your life. *"If you grasp and cling to life on your terms, you'll lose it, but if you let that life go, you'll get life on God's terms."* (Luke 17:33 MSG)

I also want to encourage you to make it a practice of speaking your "declaration of freedom." Here are a few to get you started, but you can write your own for any specific challenges you are facing.

• I am free from bondage to sin.

- I am free from guilt, shame, condemnation, anger and unforgiveness.
- I am free from debt, poverty and lack.
- I am free from sickness and disease.
- I am free from fear, anxiety and worry.
- I am free from the pain of my past.
- I am free from _____.
- I am free to become all that God created me to be.
- I am free to walk in paths of righteousness.
- I am free to soar.
- I am free to be transformed in my mind.
- I am free to _____.

You are created in the image of God who speaks of things that are presently nonexistent as though they already existed. (Romans 4:17) It may take a while for your whole being to come into agreement with the truth of your declarations, but don't stop. Eventually your faith in the finished work of the Cross will bring forth the manifestation.

My prayer for you is that you will enjoy the gift of freedom found at the Cross, guard it and use it responsibly to serve God.

PERSONAL APPLICATION

What do you need to exchange at the Cross today to experience more of the freedom that Jesus died for you to have?

_____

_____

_____

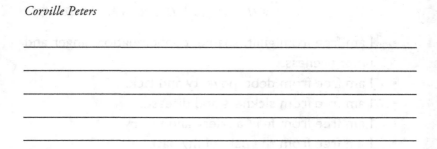

FAITH CONFESSION

At the Cross I find true freedom because Jesus has set me free.

PRAYER

Heavenly Father, thank you for your gift of freedom that I have found at the Cross. By your grace, help me to guard against the captivity of sin. Thank you for liberating me from every enslaving thought, so that my entire life can reflect the righteousness of faith through Jesus Christ and His finished work of the Cross.

A DEEPER LOOK THROUGH THE WINDOW OF TRUTH

- *Christ has freed us so that we may enjoy the benefits of freedom. Therefore, be firm [in this freedom], and don't become slaves again. (Galatians 5:1 GW)*
- *He canceled the record of the charges against us and took it away by nailing it to the cross. (Colossians 2:14 NLT)*
- *For sin shall not have dominion over you, for you are not under law but under grace. (Romans 6:14)*
- *[Live] as free people, [yet] without employing your freedom as a pretext for wickedness; but [live at all times] as servants of God. (1 Peter 2:16 AMP)*

Day 19

I receive

Victory

And having disarmed the powers and authorities,
he made a public spectacle of them, triumphing
over them by the cross.
Colossians 2:15 NIV

Did you notice the word "receive" that we've associated it with the victory of the Cross? At the Cross you receive victory! The concept of receiving victory is not the usual way of thinking about victory. Typically, we say that one has gained or won a victory, conveying the thought of contending in a battle, struggle or competition and coming out triumphant.

Well, what about the victory of the Cross? The Cross offers us the most delightful victory, because it is secured by someone else on our behalf. That is what Jesus did for us. As a man, he contended against satan and his kingdom, triumphed over him and handed us the victor's crown.

At the Cross, God demonstrated His love for us by not only redeeming us from the bondage of sin and purchasing our freedom, but He also accomplished the ultimate act of defeating satan and stripping him of all power and authority. Colossians 2:14-15 *NIV*, gives us the picture of this victorious operation.

> *"Having canceled the charge of our legal indebtedness, which stood against us and condemned us; he has taken it away, nailing it to the cross. And having disarmed the powers and authorities, he made a public spectacle of them, triumphing over them by the cross."*

My friend, this revelation will transform the way you look at your battles. Regardless of what circumstances you may face, once you are in Christ, His victory becomes your victory! This is encouraging because even when it looks as if you may be losing, you have already won. In every situation you fight the good fight of faith, knowing that you are not fighting *for* victory but *from* a position of victory.

This is what Romans 8:37 means when it says we are *"more than conquerors."* Although we did not contend in the battle, the victory has been given to us as a gift. That's not all. God displays us as a trophy of Christ's victory. If you have never thought of yourself in this manner, today is your day to start. *"But thanks be to God, Who in Christ always leads us in triumph [as trophies of Christ's victory]." (2 Corinthians 2:14 AMP)*

Experiencing and enjoying this gift of victory you received at the Cross will depend on where you direct your faith. So, be sure to anchor your faith not on what you can do in your own human strength, but on what Jesus has already done on your behalf, and on the victory He will manifest through you. The focus is all on Jesus. You and I have never been a match for satan and we will never be—except in Christ Jesus.

Temptations are a reality in our day-to-day lives and you may be wondering how to use this gift of victory in overcoming temptations. Here's how:

1. Focus your thoughts on who you are through faith in Christ Jesus. You are the righteousness of God, born anew with the divine seed of God's life in you, so activate the overcoming power of the divine life within you. (2 Corinthians 5:17, 21; 1 John 3:9)
2. Exchange your self-effort at the altar of the Cross for God's grace. (See Day 3). Learn to also use the weapons of the Word of God, as Jesus Himself did, the Blood of Jesus and the Name of Jesus. (Matthew 4:6-11; Revelation 12:11; Philippians 2:10)

Remember that when you trust in Jesus and His finished work of the Cross you are no longer under satan's dominion. You need not fear satan's tyranny or his lies. Be aware that one of his strategies is to paralyze you with fear of what the future holds. Be bold in resisting the enemy, knowing that the victory of the Cross is as powerful for today and tomorrow as it was over two thousand years ago.

PERSONAL APPLICATION

What do you need to exchange at the Cross today to experience the victory Jesus won for you?

_____

_____

_____

_____

_____

_____

_____

_____

_____

FAITH CONFESSION

Wherever I go I have victory in Jesus, my Savior forever.

PRAYER

Heavenly Father, thank you for your gift of victorious living in Jesus. I ask for your grace to help me trust the proclamation that Jesus made from the Cross: "It is finished." In every battle of life that I face, help me to remember that the only victory satan can have over me is what I allow him to have when I take my eyes off Jesus and give way to fear. By the power and might of your Holy Spirit, I will stand firmly upon your Word, believing that I have victory over every weapon the enemy tries to use against me.

A DEEPER LOOK THROUGH THE WINDOW OF TRUTH

- *But no weapon will be able to hurt you; you will have an answer for all who accuse you. I will defend my servants and give them victory." (Isaiah 54:17 GNT)*
- *They won the victory over him by the blood of the Lamb and by the truth which they proclaimed; and they were willing to give up their lives and die. (Revelation 12:11 GNT)*
- *You are of God, little children, and have overcome them, because He who is in you is greater than he who is in the world. (1 John 4:4)*

- *We are human, but we don't wage war as humans do. We use God's mighty weapons, not worldly weapons, to knock down the strongholds of human reasoning and to destroy false arguments. We destroy every proud obstacle that keeps people from knowing God. We capture their rebellious thoughts and teach them to obey Christ. (2 Corinthians 10:3-5 NLT)*
- *But thanks be to God, who gives us the victory through our Lord Jesus Christ. (2 Corinthians 15:57)*

Day 20

AT THE CROSS

I am

Restored

*Instead of shame and dishonor, you will enjoy
a double share of honor. You will possess a double
portion of prosperity in your land, and
everlasting joy will be yours.*
Isaiah 61:7 NLT

By this point in our journey of discovery I trust that you see clearly how Jesus was at work in the massive operation of the Cross restoring divine order to every area of your life. The restoration of the Cross encompasses the recovery of all that you lost, all that you relinquished by straying from God's way and all that was stolen from you as a result of satan's tyranny. Above all, through the Cross, God was at work reconciling you to Himself. (See 2 Corinthians 5:18-19)

Generation after generation since the Fall of Adam and Eve, God longed for the restoration of his human family. It was not until Jesus went to the Cross that the Father's longing was fulfilled. We see God's heart of restoration throughout the

Old Testament and today's key verse is a clear representation of the intents of His heart. Because of His great love for us, God held nothing back in accomplishing our full restoration. We understand from the promise of Isaiah 61:7 that God was after a double restoration. Today we praise God that our restoration was accomplished at the Cross.

My friend, because of the finished work of the Cross we are restored to a much better position than we would be in otherwise. Whatever trouble we experienced under the tyranny of sin, God has made provision for a double-portion restoration. This amazing blessing is available to us only through the Cross.

On Day 14 we spoke about the man named Job in the Old Testament. In some respects, he symbolizes the terror that satan brings to our lives. Job lost all his wealth, children and even his health. In the end, however, Job experienced the miraculous blessing of a double-portion restoration.

> *"And the LORD restored Job's losses when he prayed for his friends. Indeed the LORD gave Job twice as much as he had before." (Job 42:10)*

At the Cross, Jesus entered into a new covenant with God on our behalf. What this means, is that when we put our trust in the finished work of the Cross, we end up even better off than Job who was under the old covenant. The blessing of restoration you receive at the Cross is complete and it is eternal. *IT IS FINISHED!*

Although you may not presently feel or see the evidence of restoration in your life, I want to encourage you to concentrate on this key area—the presence of God. Being restored to the presence of God by the blood of Jesus shed at the Cross is the ultimate restoration. All other benefits of the Cross that we have been exploring are the means by which we are brought to this glorious end. The access that Adam and Eve lost in the Garden of Eden has been restored to us through the Cross.

Now, here is the really good news! Through the Cross, we not only have the outward access that Adam and Eve had as God met with them in the cool of the day (Genesis 3:8) we have the Spirit of God living in us.

> *"And I will pray the Father, and He will give you another Helper, that He may abide with you forever—the Spirit of truth, whom the world cannot receive, because it neither sees Him nor knows Him; but you know Him, for He dwells with you and will be in you... At that day you will know that I am in My Father, and you in Me, and I in you." (John 14:16-17, 20)*

Your restoration to the presence of God is a triple restoration, not just double—Jesus is in the Father, you are in Jesus and Jesus is in you. You will agree that restoration does not get better than that! As one restored to God's presence, you have the privilege of drawing out the restoration you need in every area of life—health, finances, relationships. You name it and it's all in His presence. The Psalmist, David, sums it up this way: *"In Your presence is fullness of joy; At Your right hand are pleasures forevermore." (Psalm 16:11)*

PERSONAL APPLICATION

What do you need to exchange at the Cross today to experience a greater dimension of restoration?

_____

_____

_____

_____

_____

_____

_____

FAITH CONFESSION

Through the finished work of the Cross, God has restored me to become and possess more than I could ever imagine or ask.

PRAYER

Heavenly Father, today we offer thanksgiving and high praises to you for the massive work of restoration you accomplished at the Cross. Thank you for holding nothing back; for giving all in love for me to be restored. I rejoice in your complete restoration, by which I have new life in Christ. By the working of your indwelling Spirit and my dwelling in your presence, from this day forward let every part of my being and life reflect the restoration I receive at the Cross.

A DEEPER LOOK THROUGH THE WINDOW OF TRUTH

- *God was using Christ to restore his relationship with humanity. He didn't hold people's faults against them, and*

> he has given us this message of restored relationships to tell others. *(2 Corinthians 5:19 GW)*

- But now in Christ Jesus you who once were far off have been brought near by the blood of Christ. Now, therefore, you are no longer strangers and foreigners, but fellow citizens with the saints and members of the household of God. *(Ephesians 2:13,19)*

- So I will restore to you the years that the swarming locust has eaten, the crawling locust, the consuming locust, and the chewing locust, My great army which I sent among you. You shall eat in plenty and be satisfied, and praise the name of the LORD your God, Who has dealt wondrously with you; and My people shall never be put to shame. Then you shall know that I am in the midst of Israel: I am the LORD your God and there is no other. My people shall never be put to shame. *(Joel 2:25-27)*

- The Spirit of the Lord is on me, because he has anointed me to proclaim good news to the poor. He has sent me to proclaim freedom for the prisoners and recovery of sight for the blind, to set the oppressed free, to proclaim the year of the Lord's favor... Today this scripture is fulfilled in your hearing. *(Luke 4:18-19, 21b NIV)*

Day 21

I have

Hope

*Now may the God of hope fill you with all joy
and peace in believing, that you may abound in hope
by the power of the Holy Spirit.*
Romans 15:13

We wrap up our Twenty-One Days at the Cross with HOPE. What kind of hope are we referring to here? Certainly not wishful thinking. Not the world's concept of hope either, which while expecting the best or a positive outcome, hedges a reservation for disappointment.

The hope of the Cross is a completely wholesome kind of hope. You see from Romans 15:13 that the hope we have in the Cross proceeds from the God of Hope and overflows by the power of the Holy Spirit. There is no disappointment in God. As Psalm 25:3 NIV says, *"No one who hopes in God will ever be put to shame."*

Hope has been described as an acronym from four words:

Having
Only
Positive
Expectations

That is truly amazing! As we have journeyed these Twenty-One Days through the meaning of the Cross, it is only fitting that we embrace this exclusively positive concept of hope.

First Corinthians 13:13 says, *"And now abide faith, hope, love, these three; but the greatest of these is love."* Indeed, the greatness of God's unfailing love demonstrated at the Cross gives us eternal hope. This great love is the source of our positive expectations and the anchor of our faith that brings forth the expectation of our hope. This is how it works: hope gives direction to your faith, and faith brings forth the manifestation of what divine love has secured for you.

Hope is absolutely essential going forward, especially when you are facing challenges and storms. So let me remind you of your *"At The Cross"* gifts and blessing that you have explored and received on this journey.

- You are LOVED and ACCEPTED.
- You have received GRACE and MERCY.
- You are FORGIVEN, CLEANSED, REDEEMED and BLESSED.
- You are BORN ANEW and MADE RIGHTEOUS.
- You are FATHERED.
- You have found FRIENDSHIP, PEACE and PROSPERITY.
- You are HEALED.

- You have find PROTECTION, SECURITY, FREEDOM and VICTORY.
- You are RESTORED with the HOPE of only God's best lavished on your life.

Your journey of discovering what the Cross means to you is by far not over. In some respects it may have just begun. My hope is that the message of the Cross has so captured your heart that you will cling to it and share its good news with others.

PERSONAL APPLICATION

What do you need to exchange at the Cross to activate hope in your daily life?

_____

_____

_____

_____

_____

_____

_____

FAITH CONFESSION

By faith in Jesus and His finished work of the Cross, I have only a positive expectation of God's goodness in my life.

PRAYER

Heavenly Father, today I praise you as the God of Hope. I pray that your hope would so fill me with complete joy and peace, as I trust wholeheartedly in you. By the power of your Holy Spirit, let my life overflow and bubble over with confident hope.

A DEEPER LOOK THROUGH THE WINDOW OF TRUTH

- *For I know the thoughts that I think toward you, says the LORD, thoughts of peace and not of evil, to give you a future and a hope. (Jeremiah 29:11)*
- *Since he did not spare even his own Son but gave him up for us all, won't he also give us everything else? (Romans 8:32 NLT)*
- *But those who wait for the Lord [who expect, look for, and hope in Him] shall change and renew their strength and power; they shall lift their wings and mount up [close to God] as eagles [mount up to the sun]; they shall run and not be weary, they shall walk and not faint or become tired. (Isaiah 40:31 AMP)*

THE WORD SERIES

THE POWER OF THE BLOOD OF JESUS

The Word Series is a collection of Scripture verses relating to the Blood of the Cross and the primary needs addressed on the broadcast of AT THE CROSS Live TV.

We encourage you to declare these verses to reinforce the power of the Cross in your life.

ACCESS TO GOD'S THRONE: *Heb. 10:19, "Therefore, brothers, since we have confidence to enter the Most Holy Place by the blood of Jesus."*

REDEEMS SLAVES OF SIN: *Rev. 5:9, "And they sang a new song: 'You are worthy to take the scroll and to open its seals, because you were slain, and with your blood you purchased men for God from every tribe and language and people and nation.'"*

PURCHASES THE CHURCH: *Acts 20:28, "Keep watch over yourselves and all the flock of which the Holy Spirit has made you overseers. Be* shepherds of the church of God, which he bought with his own blood."

MAKES PEACE BETWEEN THE RACES: *Col. 1:20, "And through him to reconcile to himself all things, whether things on earth or things in heaven, by making peace through his blood, shed on the cross."*

PROTECTS FROM THE DESTROYER: *Ex. 12:23, "When the LORD goes through the land to strike down the Egyptians, he will see the blood on the top and sides of the doorframe and will pass over that doorway, and he will not permit the destroyer to enter your houses and strike you down."*

OVERCOMES THE ACCUSER: *Rev. 12:11, "They overcame him by the blood of the Lamb and by the word of their testimony; they did not love their lives so much as to shrink from death."*

SANCTIFIES THE PEOPLE: *Heb. 13:12, "And so Jesus also suffered outside the city gate to make the people holy through his own blood."*

HEALS SICKNESS: *I Peter 2:24, "He himself bore our sins in his body on the tree, so that we might die to sins and live for righteousness; by his wounds you have been healed."*

CLEANSES FROM SIN: *I Jn. 1:7, "But if we walk in the light, as he is in the light, we have* fellowship with one another, and the blood of Jesus, his Son, purifies us from all sin."

FORGIVENESS OF SIN: *Eph. 1:7, "In him we have redemption through his blood, the forgiveness of sins, in accordance with the riches of God's grace."*

PURGES THE CONSCIENCE: *Heb. 9:14, "How much more, then, will the blood of Christ, who through the eternal Spirit offered himself unblemished to God, cleanse our consciences from acts that lead to death, so that we may serve the living God!"*

PROVIDES FELLOWSHIP BETWEEN BELIEVERS: *1 Cor. 10:16, "Is not the cup of thanksgiving for which we give thanks a participation in the blood of Christ? And is not the bread that we break a participation in the body of Christ?"*

TRIUMPHS OVER THE ENEMY: *Col. 2:15, "And having disarmed the powers and authorities, he made a public spectacle of them, triumphing over them by the cross."*

Printed in the United States
By Bookmasters